"I would buy this lovely boo
for the illustrations, and for this sent
most misunderstood of animals. Living alone in the gloom of
darkness, unsociable and virtually sightless, the mole never
gets a chance to set the record straight.'"

—Jeffrey Moussaieff Masson,
When Elephants Weep and *Dogs Never Lie About Love*

"In *Zooburbia*, Tai Moses writes with great power and
imagination about an urban wildlife corridor where humans and
animals overlap. This is a poetics of suburbia—of animals flying
above us, sharing our houses, gardens, and streets. *Zooburbia* will
delight readers who love language and will stay with them long
after they've finished reading. There is something contagious
about Moses's joy and the mindful attention she brings to her
encounters with animals. *Zooburbia* shows us that what we
consider ordinary is actually an enchanted kingdom."

—Thaisa Frank, *Enchantment* and *Heidegger's Glasses*

"While *Zooburbia* shares an extraordinary glimpse into
the natural world, it even more brilliantly gives you insight
into the human condition, and through the eyes, mind, and
heart of one of the most thoughtful, passionate, and
perceptive humans you will ever encounter."

—Thom Hartmann, *The Last Hours of Ancient Sunlight*

ZOO BURBIA

Meditations on the Wild Animals Among Us

TAI MOSES

PARALLAX
PRESS

Berkeley, California

AUTHOR'S NOTE

All of these stories are true, and all of the animals in the stories exist or existed. Identifying details and names have been changed in a few places. Some readers may wonder what dogs, horses, goldfish, and goats are doing in a book about wild animals. The answer is that all animals have a spark of wildness smoldering somewhere within.

· · ·

Parallax Press
P.O. Box 7355
Berkeley, California 94707
www.parallax.org

Parallax Press is the publishing division of Unified Buddhist Church, Inc.

Edited by Rachel Neumann
Cover and text design by Jess Morphew
Cover and interior illustrations © Dave Buchen
Author photo © Joel Moses

Library of Congress Cataloging-in-Publication Data

Moses, Tai.
    Zooburbia : meditations on the wild animals among us / Tai Moses ;
illustrated by Dave Buchen.
        pages cm
    ISBN 978-1-937006-67-9 (paperback)
    1. Human-animal relationships. 2. Self-actualization (Psychology)
I. Title.
    QL85.M68 2014
    304.2--dc23
                            2014006792

1 2 3 4 5 / 18 17 16 15 14

For MPK

Contents

One way to open your eyes is to ask yourself,
"What if I had never seen this before?
What if I knew I would never see it again?"
—Rachel Carson

At Home in Zooburbia

I like to shop at a hardware store that has an outdoor nursery where a flock of wild song sparrows lives. The store also sells sacks of birdseed, which are kept inside on shelves not far from the automatic doors. The sparrows have learned to fly in the doors as they open, snack on any spilled birdseed, and then dart back out when they're finished. It's a system that works for all, avian and human alike. Such graceful coexistence is the essence of zooburbia.

Zooburbia is what I call the extraordinary, unruly, half-wild realm where human and animal lives overlap. Within that territory lies the opportunity for some truly meaningful interspecies encounters. While zooburbia is a physical place—the cities and suburbs where our paths cross with those of other species—it's also a state of mind, the part of our psyches where animals reside, in all their many complications and contradictions.

As our cities grow and sprawl to accommodate burgeoning populations of humans, wild animals that once lived in woods and canyons and meadows are making their homes across the street from us, or even in our backyards. Modern cities are intricate ecosystems, teeming with a multitude of species that straddle the line between wild and not so wild. Raccoons that should be fishing crayfish out of woodland streams fish in garbage cans and wash their plunder in the gutter; striped skunks make their dens in storm drains and abandoned cars. Deer browse along freeway embankments. Flocks of parrots descended from escaped pets roost in sidewalk trees, and pigeons that evolved as cliff dwellers nest on window ledges. Last year I saw a wild turkey hen strolling along a downtown sidewalk, trailed by her brood of a dozen hatchlings. Traffic stopped and onlookers gawked. A handful of people seemed unnerved. But the rest of us saw the most ordinary sight in the world: a mother taking her children for a walk on a beautiful summer afternoon.

The way we think about animals is all over the map, but what is indisputable is that we *do* think about animals. Our relations with our wild neighbors can be delightful or conflicted, but they are always complex. For me, the intersection of human and animal has always been a source of wonder, and occasionally uncertainty, as I work to better understand my fellow beings and my role in their lives.

Whether wild, tame, or somewhere in between, all the animals who live among us have the capacity to enrich our lives in ways large and small. Sharing our sidewalks with wild turkeys and our shops with songbirds makes us more buoyant and more creatively connected to each other, our communities, and our planet. When we pay closer attention to the nuances of animal life we may be rewarded with a deeper connection to our own inner lives. Animals are individuals, with personalities and histories. Every one of them has a story. Zooburbia is where our stories converge.

ONE

My Green Mansions

We plan our lives according to a dream
that comes to us in our childhood,
and we find that life alters our plans.
—Ben Okri

My chief preoccupation when I was a girl growing up in the heart of Los Angeles was to find a way to get out of the city and go live alone in the wilderness with wild animals and maybe a loyal dog. The air in LA was so polluted that we had smog-alert days when kids weren't allowed to play outside. When I took a deep breath my eyes stung and my lungs burned. During recess and lunchtime we had to stay in the classroom and put our heads down on our desks to rest. I still remember how soothing that laminated surface felt against my cheek, so cool when everything else was so hot.

I knew things weren't supposed to be this way. Air was supposed to be pure and breathable. Skies should be clear and blue, not hazy and orange. Rivers weren't supposed to be sheathed in concrete, their bends straightened and rapids muzzled. With a freeway on one side and railroad tracks on the other, the Los Angeles River was as eager to escape its concrete prison as I was to escape the city. Cattails, rushes, and reeds took root in the riverbed; tiny green frogs hopped up and down the algaed banks. In the rainy season, torrents of muddy water thundered down the channel, sweeping along shopping carts, tree trunks, tires, and sometimes even an unfortunate person.

I dreamed of woods, creeks, and mountains. I dreamed of wild animals and of wildness—wildness in the true sense of the word, untamed and free. At the public library, I haunted the nature section, checking out books that taught me the names of birds and mammals, flowers and trees. I memorized animal tracks and cloud formations. Certain words ignited fiery particles in my imagination: *Prairie. Forest. Grizzly. Waterfall. Mustang. Eagle. Arroyo.* I loved the very sound and shape of these words. I pored over my dog-eared copy of *How To Stay Alive in the Woods.*[1] I even assembled my own moccasins with a kit I got from the Tandy Leather Factory.

I planned to live in a lean-to, or a hollowed-out tree, like the boy in the novel *My Side of the Mountain.*[2] Unlike that boy, I wouldn't hunt to survive. I would eat wild forest plants and fruits and seeds, and I would befriend wild animals and birds.

---

[1]   Bradford Angier, *How to Stay Alive in the Woods* (New York: Black Dog and Leventhal Publishers, 2001). Bradford Angier's classic book was inspired by the principles of self-reliance modeled by Henry Thoreau.

[2]   Jean Craighead George, *My Side of the Mountain* (New York: Puffin Books, 2004).

My model for living peaceably among wild creatures came from another novel: *Green Mansions* by William H. Hudson.[3]

Green Mansions, published in 1904, is set in turn-of-the-century Venezuela. A young adventurer named Abel journeys deep into the jungle, where he meets a mysterious girl named Rima. Rima is the sole survivor of a peaceful, vegetarian tribe that was wiped out by disease and warfare. She has a voice like birdsong and can communicate with birds in their own language. Her dresses are spun from spider silk. Rima will neither harm animals nor eat them, and when men come to the forest to hunt, she hurls their poison-tipped arrows back at them from the trees.

Abel falls in love with this "wild, solitary girl of the woods" and wants to bring her back to the city of Caracas with him, but Rima refuses to leave her home. The story ends horribly. A mob of fearful natives who believe Rima is a witch chases her into the jungle. She climbs up into an enormous tree where she thinks she will be safe, surrounded by her beloved birds and animals, but the natives set the tree on fire, and Rima the bird girl is burned to death.

I was devastated by the ending of her story. It wasn't until I was older that I understood Hudson's message: that fear and ignorance are a plague upon humanity; that weapons and technology can crush the human soul; that a tenderhearted idealist like Rima was not meant to live in our pitiless modern world.

When I did finally go live in the forest, it wasn't to the wilderness exactly, but to Yosemite Valley. I was seventeen,

---

3   William H. Hudson, *Green Mansions*, available online at: eldritchpress.org/whh/gmans.htm.

the same age as Rima the bird girl. I had dropped out of high school a year early, but I'd passed the California high school proficiency exam, which asserted that I had the knowledge of a graduate. Still, one had to be eighteen to get a job, so with the help of a bottle of Wite-Out, a copy machine, and my portable typewriter, I made myself a new birth certificate and I was hired to work in the cafeteria at Yosemite Lodge.

* * *

At work I wore an institutional brown and orange uniform with brown kneesocks, and stood behind the steam table dishing out meatloaf to tourists. When I wasn't at work, I explored the park. The dogwoods were in bloom and the waterfalls were thundering. The ice-streaked granite, the rippling meadows filled with purple lupines, and the aroma of crushed pine needles underfoot all made me dizzy with happiness. I went backpacking and saw my first wild black bear, my first marmot, and my first alpine lake. For the first time, I saw a night sky brimming over with stars.

Every week I would hitchhike up to a little meadow I'd discovered a half hour away from the valley. I never saw another human in that meadow. Deer browsed at the edges of the woods and birds busied themselves in the trees. I'd brought my *New Oxford Book of American Verse* with me from Los Angeles, and I'd stretch out in the shade and read for hours.[4] When I was done with that, I read anything I could get my hands

---

4   *The New Oxford Book of American Verse* (New York: Oxford University Press, 1976).

on, borrowed, bought, or traded. When the shadows began to lengthen and a chill crept into the air, I'd walk back to the road, put my thumb out and hitch a ride down to the valley floor. Years later, when people asked me where I went to college, I always thought of that meadow—my green mansion—and everything I'd learned within its leafy green walls. I was a long way from being Rima the bird girl, but something in Yosemite satisfied my longing for wildness, beauty, and peace.

* * *

Today, I live in a city again, a different city that I see with new eyes. T. S. Eliot wrote that, "the end of all our exploring will be to arrive where we started and know the place for the first time."[5] I know that animals are always among us, just as we are always in nature. Instead of looking for those treasured qualities of beauty, peace, and wildness in a distant and idealized wilderness, I try to carry them with me wherever I go. And sometimes I wonder: maybe Rima the bird girl could have survived in Caracas. Maybe she could have found enough beauty and birdsong to nourish and sustain herself, as I have slowly learned to do, and maybe in that way she could have lived.

---

5   T. S. Eliot, "Little Gidding," *Four Quartets* (New York: Mariner Books, 1968).

TWO

Conditions for Happiness

Nature is not a place to visit. It is home.
—Gary Snyder

There are certain things I can count on in this life: a cream-colored cat asleep in a bed of eucalyptus bark at the top of the hill where the morning sun first strikes the earth; mourning doves silhouetted on the bare branches of my neighbor's plum tree on a November afternoon; and a flock of golden-crowned sparrows scratching for seeds under the black sage, whistling *Oh dear me, I'm so cheery.*

Then there are the surprises. On a blustery day last winter a flock of migrating cedar waxwings descended on the cotoneaster in my backyard with the manic energy of a tempest. Hundreds of sleek gray birds with lemony chests covered the tree, devouring berries, passing berries to other birds who couldn't reach them, darting and swooping with startling speed and grace.

One night after seeing a movie downtown with friends, I was standing under the streetlights about to get in my car when I looked up into a tree filled with night herons. A tattoo parlor was on one corner, a bail bondsman was on the other, and here in the middle was a congregation of blue-gray shore-birds roosting like feathered fruit in a sidewalk tree.

I looked out my kitchen window one morning and saw three young deer bounding across the hillside behind my house, their bodies dappled with the sunlight filtering through the eucalyptus trees. Back and forth they raced, coursing with energy, vaulting and twisting as they vied to outdo each other with ever-higher leaps. Their exuberance was infectious—I could feel it flooding my body, expanding the boundaries of my heart. Something inside me burns a little brighter when animals are around.

* * *

I live at the foot of the foothills, at the end of a dead-end street in a woodsy ravine less than five miles from downtown Oakland, California. My home abuts a fan-shaped expanse of undeveloped land, brushy hillside studded with oaks and topped with eucalyptus. The hillside is a dry landscape, carpeted with eucalyptus bark and oak leaf litter. The sun spills down the hill into a little pocket-sized native meadow in my backyard. Bordered by streets on all sides, this wooded sanctuary in the midst of the city supports deer, raccoons, squirrels, opossums, skunks, moles, lizards, wild turkeys and innumerable species of birds, butterflies, bees, and other insects.

I have come to recognize several of my wild neighbors by sight. I know the huge mama raccoon who trails a new litter of kits behind her every year, often accompanied by one or two elder siblings from a previous litter. I know the pair of red-tailed hawks who nest in the tallest eucalyptus and whose shrill rasping cries I hear daily as they ride the thermals over my house. I know the timid feral cats who haunt the fringes of the neighborhood. I know the colonies of Western scrub-jays and Steller's jays, tribal birds who scold and chatter as they claim ownership of this piece of sky or that tree.

I know the twin skunks who were orphaned while still the size of softballs, barely able to fend for themselves. They appeared one night, sauntering onto the deck to gobble down the last morsels of kibble in a bowl I had set out for a feral cat. When the tiny skunks arrived, the cat stepped aside, feigning indifference as the skunks finished her meal. A raccoon showed up, but the skunks were unfazed, presenting their luxuriant tails to the raccoon as they continued to munch the kibble. When the skunks grew a little older I stopped feeding them, and for a few nights the two would march up to the glass door and peer indignantly inside with their nearsighted eyes.

Another night there was a new visitor, a young opossum who had somehow lost half his scaly tail. Opossums use their prehensile tails as a sort of extra hand when climbing trees or scaling fences, so this handicap would make life more difficult for this little guy.

I have developed relationships of a sort with these animals, even if the relationships are a bit one-sided. I recognize them; I care about them. Recently I saw the huge buck who is the leader of the little band of black-tailed deer that make their home in my neighborhood. The buck's knee was hugely swollen and there was a cut on his neck. His bloody scrapes and injured leg tell a story, though it is one I can only guess at. Was he sideswiped by a car, caught on a fence? I worry about him, but all I can do is watch and wonder as he holds his antlered head high and limps through my backyard and up the stairway. Perhaps wild animals do not need us as much as we think they do.

One Anna's Hummingbird has been hanging around for a couple of weeks. With their hollow bones, elongated bills, and brilliant patterns, hummingbirds seem to have coevolved along with the flowers. Their wings beat in a figure-eight pattern so the tiny birds can hover while they dip their grooved tongues deep into the center of a blossom to lap up the nectar. This single hummingbird may visit more than a thousand flowers a day.

Whenever I look outside, Anna is perched atop the feeder, facing north, wind ruffling her feathers. She stays until the last possible minute, until the sky begins to darken and she has to fly off to wherever hummingbirds spend the night. One day after taking a sip from the feeder, Anna flew back up to her perch and faced south, and it was then I discovered her secret: she had only one eye.

Observing these wild creatures has helped me to cultivate the habit of mindful attention. This wasn't something I set out to do; it's a consequence of sharing my space with animals and of my joy in their presence. The hawk flies overhead and my heart lifts almost as if I am up there soaring with her. A procession of wild turkeys makes their way along the deer path and I feel gratitude for their beauty. A monarch butterfly floats through my backyard, the first one of the season. Buddhists say that the conditions for happiness are always present in our lives, if we can learn to recognize them. The hawk, the wild turkey, and the monarch butterfly are my conditions for happiness.

* * *

On an early fall afternoon, the last bit of light fades from the day, leaving pink and amber clouds. The first rain of the winter comes on the autumnal equinox, a steadily falling rain, tapping on the pane, falling on the muddy hillside, and streaking the trunks of the trees. This is real rain: pouring, pelting, slashing, driving, sluicing-off-the-roofs, streaming-down-your-face, puddling-in-the-curbs, snails-on-the-sidewalk rain. After a long dry summer the birds are ecstatic, flitting through the drops and chirruping in the trees. Even the squirrels seem to rejoice, and I rejoice with them. The rain lets up, leaving the trees dripping, the bees slumbering inside the petals of a flower, and the sparrows singing. The yellow flowers glisten. The birds huddle deeper into the oak.

A small stone Buddha sits on a stump halfway up the hillside. He watches the raccoons and the orphaned skunks, the opossum with half a tail, the one-eyed hummingbird, the band of black-tailed deer, the finches and the chickadees, the towhees and the jays, the lizards and spiders, the cats and the humans. Some live and some die, some eat and others are eaten. Through it all, the Buddha is impartial. A shower of eucalyptus bark falls on his head. A line of ants marches across his lap. A feral cat curls around his sun-warmed stone back. A jay perches on the Buddha's head. The Buddha is patient. He's happy to spend eternity on his stump, while the birds peck his stone head and the rain falls in his stone lap. He's content with the day and content with the night. He is content when the sun is shining and when it's not. He is the one constant amid all the change.

THREE

Making Salad for Deer

hen I first moved to the lower hills of Oakland, to this house with its flat backyard encircled by an amphitheater of trees, the first thing on my mind was that I could finally satisfy my hankering to be a backyard farmer. I had been reading vegetable-gardening books for months, and when planting season arrived, I was ready. There was already a raised bed in the backyard. I put in a second raised bed and I planted a huge vegetable garden. I put in tomatoes and sunflowers. I erected a bean teepee. I grew herbs and lettuces, carrots and squash, and I bought a home composter.

Perhaps inevitably, chicken fever struck. I started reading books about raising chickens. I perused online chicken forums and I researched chicken feed. I ordered a chicken coop from the UK—a special coop designed for urban chicken keepers. When I went to pick up the coop at the Greyhound bus station, a woman wheeled a large flat box out on a trolley. I blurted out in excitement, "It's a chicken coop!"

She rolled her eyes. "Oh honey, I got chicken coops all day long. They started comin' about six months ago. Red ones, blue ones ... what's this one?" She peered at the cardboard box through the bottom of her bifocals, "Huh. Green."

* * *

On Saturday my husband and I picked up our three chickens, and on the way home we stopped at a deli for a quick lunch. We parked in the shade and left the chickens in a dog kennel in the car. I thrilled to the sound of their soft soothing clucks. Inside the deli, Michael scanned the menu. "Chicken salad, grilled chicken sandwich, chicken vegetable soup." He hesitated.

"I'll have a tuna sandwich," he told the cashier.

At home I installed the chickens in their new coop. During the day I allowed them out of the coop to forage. I had anticipated supreme levels of chicken happiness as the chickens rummaged in the wood chips in the backyard, but the three pullets seemed most interested in peering into the house. They would stand on the deck and watch us through the sliding glass doors.

"Go eat some snails," I said to the chickens, shooing them away.

But these chickens wouldn't eat snails. I couldn't believe it. All my research had led me to believe that chickens loved snails and slugs. The chickens preferred cracked corn. They adored yogurt. The slugs set themselves to devouring my beans with enthusiasm. Every night, I went outside with a flashlight and a jar of soapy water and picked slugs off the beans. I harvested dozens and dozens of plump slimy slugs. My animosity toward the slugs became so pronounced I could hardly sleep at night for imagining all the damage the slugs were doing as they chewed their way through my lovingly tended garden. I had read somewhere that the average garden had five thousand slugs, and that for every slug I captured, twenty more were hiding in the crevices.

I started to get discouraged the morning I discovered that squirrels had eaten the sunflowers down to the ground and deer had devoured the tomato vines—not just the fruit, but the leaves and stalks. I erected a spindly mesh fence around my raised beds to keep the animals out. When I went outside to water one morning, I noticed that something had been eating the chard. Several leaves had ragged, bitten edges. I picked a leaf, put it in a baggie and took it to the nursery where a nurseryman identified the perpetrator as a caterpillar.

"But I haven't seen any caterpillars," I said.

He said he wasn't surprised. "Caterpillars can be kind of hard to see."

"What do you recommend?"

He handed me a small bottle labeled Caterpillar Killer. "This works very well," he said. "You spray it on the leaves and a few days after the caterpillar feeds, its stomach explodes."

That seemed extreme to me. I did not want to use any chemicals in my garden, and besides, what would this substance do to the hapless bird who ate the caterpillar?

"Do you have anything less lethal?" I asked.

He showed me a natural insect repellant made from garlic juice, though he didn't have much to say about it. I bought it anyway. You have to make the kind of world you want to live in, and in my world I'd rather have caterpillars with garlic breath than exploding caterpillars.

Meanwhile, the raccoons had detected the irresistible fragrance of live chicken wafting over the backyard. I was consumed with fear that a raccoon would get its questing hand inside the coop at night. Internet chicken forums were full of ghastly stories describing what a raccoon could do to a chicken, or any part of a chicken it could reach.

* * *

One day, I watched a doe delicately nibble the petals off each of the wild yellow irises that had just bloomed on the hillside. I knew I should chase the deer away, but after a day of cleaning out the chicken coop, composting and weeding, and on the heels of another late-night slug-hunting expedition, I was too exhausted to get up. Also, I found that I didn't really care. Watching the doe eat the flowers, I imagined how sweet the petals must taste, and for the first time in a long while I felt something like peace. Sometimes you have to let things fall apart. They're going to anyway.

I had grown weary of my horticultural battles. I was tired of living in opposition to the wild animals who inhabited this land. As I started to pay closer attention to the environment around me, I saw the unwritten natural history of the land upon which I was living. I saw the deer paths that meandered through the neighborhood. I saw the fallen trees and piles of brush where animals denned, the crevices in the rock wall where lizards sunned themselves, the cavities in trees where birds nested. Everywhere I looked I saw tracks and signs. I heard calls and songs.

This was an urban wildlife corridor where animals had lived for decades, probably centuries. They were the descendants of animals that had long-established watering, feeding, and denning areas in this neighborhood. This land belonged to the deer and raccoons and skunks, the squirrels and opossums, the songbirds and mourning doves, the hawks and owls, the lizards and the spiders. The animals were marooned here on this forested oasis, hemmed in by a network of streets and freeways. They had been pushed to the margins as humans built homes on top of their homes and destroyed the plants and trees and streams that had always nourished them. I had other ways to get my food; the animals didn't.

I found my three chickens a new home where they could free-range all day and no one would force them to eat snails. Despite the feverish amount of energy I had expended in getting, and then in keeping these chickens, I found it was not hard to part with them. Deep down, perhaps I knew they never really belonged here. I sold my lime-green chicken coop to another eager urban chicken keeper. I tore out the two raised beds and recycled the lumber, and I put my vegetable gardening books on a high shelf. I had a different vision in mind now. I would help sustain my wild neighbors by cultivating the habitat they needed to thrive.

FOUR

Rat Race

I was walking around Lake Merritt in Oakland when I saw a man sitting on a bench snuggling a small spotted dog. As I got closer I saw that my eyes had deceived me: the man was holding an armful of rats. Five of them were nestled in the crook of his arm, lined up in a neat row, eyes closed and tails dangling like strings. The whole scene was very peaceful.

"May I pet one of your rats?" I asked. The man handed me a brown and white rat. She opened her eyes and regarded me drowsily, and I stroked her sleek head. Her ears were translucent seashells. She smelled sweet. Rats groom themselves constantly, and the fur of a clean rat has a fresh, woodsy scent.

"These are very nice rats," I said.

The man nodded. "They enjoy the fresh air," he said. Small and wiry, the man was pleasantly ratlike himself, with his neat, angular features and short, dark hair.

I tickled the rat's silken belly and her whiskers twitched. I have always been fond of rats and mice. They are highly social animals, inquisitive and keenly intelligent. Whenever I am in a hardware store and I pass the "pest control" aisle, I always hide the cruel glue traps and rat poisons behind the boxes of leaf bags so that people can't find them.[6]

"Would you like to sit down?" the man asked.

I hesitated. It was one thing to stand there and pet an anonymous rat for a moment. But if I sat down, the man and I would have to talk to each other. What would we say to each other? Would it be awkward? I often find myself going though these mental calculations: *How long will I have to talk? What will I say? When can I leave?* The shyness and discomfort I frequently feel around humans is absent when I am with animals. With animals, I feel at home. At parties, I can often be found petting the family dog in the backyard or trying to coax the cat out of the guest room. The company of animals is both stimulating and soothing; a way to suspend the demands of language while still enjoying the nearness of another mind.

I looked longingly at the rats burrowed under the man's arm, their tiny paws grasping the fabric of his jacket. Something told me the ratman was a kindred spirit. I perched on the edge of the bench. The man scooped up the brown and white rat and offered me a glossy gray rat. The gray rat sat up

---

[6]   Rodenticides are lethal to many other animals besides wild rats and mice: they also kill owls, hawks, bobcats, foxes, mountain lions, dogs, cats, and any other animal that eats the flesh of the poisoned rat. Learn more at raptorsarethesolution.org.

on his hind legs and reached out with his front paws, like a small child asking to be picked up, and I obliged. He climbed up on my shoulder and seemed fascinated by my earring, which was shiny and silver. He kept patting it gently, interrogatively, until the ratman warned me that the gray rat had a collection of shiny things in his cage at home and if I didn't watch out, my earring would become part of it. I lifted the gray rat off my shoulder and onto my lap, where he nestled in my cupped hands.

I once read that Helen Keller could recognize people and discern their temperaments and moods by their hands. What a sighted person might read in a face—grief, gladness, fear— she sensed from the touch of a hand. "Not only is the hand as easy to recognize as the face, but it reveals its secrets more openly and unconsciously," she wrote.[7] Rats have a highly developed sense of touch. Perhaps the rat, too, could read a hand. I wondered what secrets my hand revealed. Did this trusting rat know that my kind had set out to kill his kind using some of the most noxious poisons ever conceived? Did he know that his very name, *rat*, was synonymous with the lowest members of human society: *sleazeball, lowlife, scoundrel, wretch, fink, snitch, creep, scumbag?* I hoped this guilty knowledge could not percolate through my hand. Just in case, I tried to think positive thoughts.

I sat back on the bench and let myself breathe more deeply. I was glad I had accepted the man's offer to sit. When you've been in constant motion, even a few moments of stillness can

---

7   Helen Keller, *The World I Live In* (New York: New York Review of Books Classics, 2004).

feel like buoyancy. I couldn't remember the last time I had sat with another human without talking or doing anything.

I had always thought of rats as fidgety, but these rats were calm. They seemed content to rest in the shade. As I gently stroked the top of the gray rat's head, I noticed the glassy surface of the lake and the snowy egret standing motionless at the edge, its gaze focused on the water. The ever-present anxieties that scurry about in the back of my mind began to swim away, like silvery fish scattering into the depths when a pebble falls into the water.

"Did you know that rats can laugh?" the ratman asked. He told me about a neuroscientist who had discovered that rats tickle each other during play and make a joyful sound at a pitch too high for the human ear to detect.[8] Not only are the rats ticklish only on certain parts of their bodies, their high-frequency chirps are equivalent to human laughter, a clear sign the rats have a complex emotional life that includes joy. I pictured the neuroscientist working long days in his laboratory tickling rats, trying to discover the exact location on their small bodies that would elicit a supersonic giggle—armpit, ear, belly?

"It doesn't surprise me," the ratman said of the study. "My rats are very emotional. And love seems to be their dominant emotion."

The gray rat was watching me attentively. I could feel his rat consciousness, the piercing intelligence behind those black eyes. Wordlessly, with sensations far more acute than ours,

---

[8]   Jaak Panksepp, "Beyond a Joke: From Animal Laughter to Human Joy," *Science* (April 2005).

rats perceive the world without the shadings of opinion and judgment that humans bring to each moment. What would it be like to live with such clarity, to feel pure curiosity, pure hunger, pure joy? I imagine it would be like swimming in a lake where the water is so clear you can make out discrete grains of sand on the bottom. Every communication would be transparent. We would tickle each other with joyful affection and fall asleep in a heap, our bodies curled together for warmth and comfort. It would be a world in which *rat* means *laugh, play, happy, tickle, yes.*

The ratman handed me a plastic bag full of green peas and I offered one to the gray rat. He took the pea and popped it into his mouth. He ate several more peas. Then, cleaning his pointy face with his paws, the rat yawned, showing off his buckteeth, curled up on my lap and fell asleep. All around us, walkers, runners, bicyclists, rollerbladers, and stroller-pushing parents thronged the path, talking, chatting on cell phones, or listening to music through earphones, everybody briskly charging forward, trying to get ahead of the rat race.

FIVE

How to Make a Forest

If we start sharing our landscapes with other living things,
we should be able to save much of the biodiversity that still exists.
—Douglas Tallamy

Years ago, I met a butterfly farmer in Maui. She and her husband owned some land on the flanks of Mount Haleakala where they raised swallowtail, monarch, and Gulf fritillary butterflies. They had so many butterflies that they released the extras to flutter around the property pollinating all the flowering tropical plants. There were butterflies indoors too, perched on the bathroom towel rack, getting a sip of water at the kitchen faucet, clinging to the bedroom curtains. The butterfly farmer told me she'd gotten so used to seeing butterflies that if she opened her eyes in the morning and didn't see a butterfly, she worried that something was wrong.

I've thought about that remark many times over the years, because I too have come to believe that when I don't see a butterfly—or a bee, a beetle, or a bird—something is deeply wrong. Like frogs, native bees, and songbirds, monarchs and other species of butterflies are disappearing from our environment as their habitat is developed and the host plants they depend upon for survival are replaced by exotic plants that do not sustain butterflies, or any other insect, for that matter. All the gardeners I know say they see fewer butterflies, and fewer insects of all kinds, every year. People who have their hands in the soil on a regular basis notice these kinds of things.

For decades, we have been systematically eliminating the food sources insects need to survive—namely, the native vegetation that occurs naturally in whatever place you live. Species of native plants have coevolved with the insects over thousands of years. The native plants feed the bugs and the birds, and in turn the bugs and birds pollinate the plants or help distribute their seeds, thereby participating in one of the earth's most fundamental rituals of cooperation. Virtually all birds, except sea birds, depend on insects for food. Birds cannot survive on seeds and berries alone. Baby songbirds eat nothing *but* insects. Dwindling insects means dwindling birds.

The most crucial thing I learned in all of my reading and studying and conversations with far wiser and more experienced wildlife gardeners was this: *native plants are the irreplaceable foundations of life*. When we remove native plants from our landscapes and replace them with roads and parking lots and lawns and exotic shrubs, we create havoc in the natural world. Without native plants, there will be no native butterflies or insects and without insects there will be no frogs, toads, snakes, lizards, birds, bats, raccoons, bobcats, deer, and on up the food chain to humans. Declining populations of butterflies and wild bees are a sign of that slow-motion disaster-in-progress. City and suburban gardens that are carpeted with lawns and colorful ornamental shrubs and flowers may look lush and inviting, but they are practically devoid of nutrition for insects and birds.

* * *

Learning all of this made everything much simpler for me. One of the most important things I could do to help my wild neighbors was to restore native habitat—to support the right kinds of growing things, remove some of the harmful things, and then stand back and allow nature to flourish. The entomologist and ecologist Douglas Tallamy writes that, "gardeners have become important players in the management of our nation's wildlife. It is now within the power of individual gardeners to do something that we all dream of doing: to make a difference."[9]

There were already many native shrubs growing on the hillside behind my home, so I planted several more in my backyard. I put a birdbath where the tomato cages once stood. The level space where the two raised beds used to be became a small meadow of native bunch grasses commingled with wildflowers like poppies and asters.

There had always been jays and towhees on the hillside, but I began to see far more species. I counted goldfinches,

---

9   Douglas W. Tallamy, *Bringing Nature Home: How You Can Sustain Wildlife with Native Plants* (Portland, OR: Timber Press, 2009).

juncos, chickadees, and bushtits. Downy woodpeckers were regular visitors. I saw my first ruby-crowned kinglet. Cabbage white, skippers, and swallowtail butterflies fluttered over the meadow grasses. On summer afternoons, when the sun slipped behind the hillside and shade crept over the meadow, I would go outside and marvel at all the buzzing, flying, flitting, cheeping, singing life.

Sharing my environment with wildlife meant relinquishing some control, which I found liberating. Instead of trying to outwit nature and sneak a harvest of exotic vegetables under its nose, I now felt that we were allies. Gardening for wildlife gave me permission to be untidy and imperfect. It was a relief to abandon the perfectionist tendencies that had caused me so much torment. The less I compulsively raked, groomed, and tidied up my garden, the more likely it was that birds and wildlife would find nourishment and shelter there. Instead of deadheading flowers, I left them on the stalks as food for finches and sparrows. A volunteer bush of oregano was growing in a corner of the garden. I ignored it, letting it grow tall and spindly, and when it flowered, its white blossoms were covered in ecstatic bees from morning to night.

I used to be annoyed when I saw bites taken out of the leaves in my garden. But leaf damage could also be a sign of the presence of caterpillar larvae, which would soon became the butterfly or moth whose beauty I so enjoyed. Ladybugs, butterflies, and bees made their winter homes in wilted flower stalks, and drifts of fallen leaves were mulch for trees. A pile of dead vegetation in the corner of the yard made a cozy shelter for lizards and other small creatures. As the vegetation decomposed, it provided food and nutrients for the soil and for the next generation of growing things.

* * *

As our planet's prairies, forests, and wetlands shrink, our city and suburban gardens, no matter what size they are, can do a lot to help rescue many species from the brink. Collectively, the patchwork mosaic of our backyards, front yards, decks, terraces, rooftops, balconies, community gardens, sidewalk planters, vacant lots, and median strips adds up to a tremendous amount of habitat—a lot of places for weary, migrating songbirds and butterflies to find a bite to eat and a place to rest.

In the face of climate change and widespread habitat loss, the gardener-poet Benjamin Vogt says that gardening has become an ethical act. "Choosing native plants may be a moral choice," he writes. "Asking for them in nurseries is asking for change, for restoration, for healing."[10]

If you plant a tub of milkweed on your little apartment terrace and a monarch butterfly finds it and lays her eggs, you have just lodged a protest against the forces that would cover our world with concrete; that would fill our rivers and streams with chemicals; that would lay waste to our forests and cut the tops off our mountains. Tearing out your lawn and planting a native oak and a meadow of native grasses and wildflowers is an inspired way to repudiate the giant pesticide and lawn-care industries that still spray with abandon many

---

[10]   Benjamin Vogt, "Native Plants Are a Moral Choice": gardenrant.com

of the life-destroying chemicals Rachel Carson warned us about more than half a century ago."

The same measures that safeguard our wild neighbors also enrich our human communities. When neighbors agree not to use rat poisons to protect nesting hawks and owls, or to forgo the use of pesticides and herbicides to protect bees, butterflies, and songbirds, these decisions benefit not just wildlife, but children, pets, and every other living thing. By preserving or restoring native habitat around our homes, not only do we get to enjoy the beauty of the natural landscape, we support the web of biodiversity that enables all species, including our own, to survive. We experience the joy of giving something back to this earth that has given us so much.

---

11   Rachel Carson, *Silent Spring* (New York: Houghton Mifflin, 2002).

SIX

The Mindfulness Bull

To pay attention, this is our endless and proper work.
—Mary Oliver

I've always been a great daydreamer. I woolgather and mind-wander, and generally forget to pay attention to what's going on around me. Once I was making tea, leaning against the stove and waiting for the kettle to boil. It took me a few moments to notice the flames licking at my shirttail. My thoughts were in one world, while my body, even ablaze, was in another.

Minor mishaps like that were not infrequent in my life. I burned toast and overflowed the bathtub; I missed my train stop or freeway exit. Yet I found it difficult to give up daydreaming. There was always so much to think about in the playground of my imagination.

Then one day in early spring, I went for a ramble in a regional park up in the foothills. I was wandering through a grassy valley, adrift in a pleasant reverie, when I came upon a herd of cows grazing along the path. A large, glossy, black cow raised its head and looked at me, but I continued to stroll absentmindedly down the path. When I was a few cow's nose-lengths from the black cow, it dawned on me that this was not a cow at all, but a bull.

The bull, now undeniably a bull, lowered his head, pawed the ground, and two cartoon puffs of steam issued from his nostrils. His breath smelled herbaceous and slightly malty. I froze. I racked my brain trying to remember what to do when faced with an irate bull. Was I supposed to make myself appear larger by shouting and waving my arms around? Or should I try to seem smaller, perhaps even play dead? Should I climb a tree, dive into a river, run like hell? Then I thought, *I'll just sidle by; he won't even notice me.* I took one cautious step forward. The bull sashayed over—I was amazed at how quickly this massive animal could move—and butted me in the side, and I bounced across the path as effortlessly as a pebble.

Heart hammering, I scrambled to my feet and scurried away down the path. I looked over my shoulder to see if the bull was in pursuit, but he was ignoring me, enthusiastically cropping the grass where I had been standing. A thought went through my mind as clearly as if a voice had spoken in my ear: *Wake up!* And at that moment, I did feel remarkably, spectacularly awake. Adrenaline can have that effect on a person. The grass looked greener, the sky more cerulean. Had birdsong always sounded this melodious? Had acorns always had this marvelous conical shape, this satiny shell? Fully awake and engaged in the present moment, I felt like a new kind of animal: a mindful one. The bull had shaken and awakened me into a heightened state of awareness and it felt . . . wonderful.

I looked back at the herd. Some of the cows were settled down on the grass chewing their cud and gazing off into the middle distance, though I knew they were also alert and watchful, aware of any danger that might come their way. They were ruminating—consciously. I thought of the way my dog sometimes lies on the couch in a sphinx-like posture, her paws crossed in front of her, eyes half-closed, ears pricked. She appears to be dozing, yet her senses are fully engaged. Cats spend hours in the same intermediate state, projecting a sense of absolute calm while remaining intently aware of their environment. Perhaps the practice of mindfulness was an attempt to mirror the attentive yet meditative states so many animals slip into naturally when they are at rest.

At the beginning and the end of formal Buddhist meditation sessions, someone typically rings a bell. Zen master Thich Nhat Hanh says the sound of the bell is the Buddha's way of reminding us to come home to ourselves—in other words, to bring our attention into the present moment. "You have an appointment with life—you should not miss it," he says. "The time and the space of your appointment is the here and the now."[12] He says anything can be a mindfulness bell: the ringing of a phone, the barking of a dog, a traffic light— even, I suppose, a two-ton bull.

I felt grateful to the bull who had knocked me over and brought me home to myself. The bull had actually shown great restraint, using no more force than necessary to remove

---

[12]   Thich Nhat Hanh, "Transforming Negative Habit Energies," *The Mindfulness Bell*, (Summer 2000, issue No. 26).

me from his salad bar. I still daydream, but I also try to practice conscious rumination, my beastly form of mindfulness. Someday, I hope to be as skilled as the bull, standing calmly in the shade, swishing his tail at the flies, chewing his cud and ruminating on his inner world, aware of all that is within and all that is without.

SEVEN

Becoming Unafraid

Perhaps everything that frightens us is,
in its deepest essence,
something helpless that wants our love.
—Rainer Maria Rilke

For years I had a recurring nightmare: I'm asleep in my bed when I open my eyes and see the silhouette of a man standing at my bedside. He doesn't speak or move. He just stares at me, mute and menacing, looming over me in the night.

After years of waking up screaming from this dream, it occurred to me that maybe the wordless figure at my bedside didn't intend to harm me at all. Perhaps this silent, suffering being needed my help. I decided that next time the dream came, I wouldn't scream; instead, I would reach out and ask the man if I could help him. But I never had the dream again.

I thought of this dream the day my cat, Puck, brought me a large and hairy spider. The spider was the size of my fist and very much alive. I was sitting on the deck when Puck dropped the spider at my feet before quickly stepping back—perhaps even he was a little alarmed by its size. I ran into the house and closed the door, staring at the spider from behind the safety of the glass. The giant spider sat motionless. It looked very small next to Puck, who was curiously tapping it with a forepaw. This spider wasn't going to hurt me; it needed my help. I went out and grabbed Puck, and brought him back into the house so the spider could recover from its ordeal and return to its burrow, wherever it was, in peace and safety.

I brought my laptop over to the kitchen table so I could keep an eye on the spider. A quick Internet search revealed it was a species called *Calisoga longitarsus*, common to the Oakland hills and known as a false tarantula because it so closely resembles the real thing. I learned that Calisoga is silvery gray instead of black like a true tarantula, and that females usually stay home in their dens while males are frequently seen in the fall roaming around in search of a mate. It was October, so my spider was probably a male. My friend Calisoga was not poisonous to humans, "although they will bite if molested."[13] I didn't hold that against the spider. It seemed reasonable to bite if someone was molesting you.

Knowing the spider's name and some of his natural history made me feel a little warmer toward him. I went out on the deck and forced myself to examine Calisoga more closely. I studied his furred and spindly legs. The rounded tips of his feet looked like silvery ballet slippers. I looked at his eyes, or what I thought were his eyes. Though I did not find him beautiful, I could see that another spider might. The longer I stood there calmly observing the spider, the less skittish I felt.

---

[13] SaveNature.org

Calisoga moved his two front legs, questing, cautiously reaching forward. He slowly crawled to the edge of the deck and then walked out into the yard and around the corner. I watched him until he was out of sight. I hoped he was successful in his search for a spouse, although I also hoped the happy couple would decide to set up housekeeping on the hillside a little farther away from my house.

* * *

I had been afraid of spiders my whole life. My fear felt like an old story I'd lived with for so long I couldn't even remember the source. Watching Calisoga crawl away, I felt deeply tired of being afraid of spiders. When I gave it some more thought, I realized I was not afraid a spider would hurt me; I rarely worried about that. I liked and respected spiders. I thought they were interesting and beneficial, and their webs can be beautiful. I just didn't like being too near them and I was afraid of having one crawl on me. My fear, then, seemed purely a reflex, a physical reaction to a spider's presence. What would happen if I decided not to react?

The Buddhist teacher Sylvia Boorstein writes that, "Fearlessness comes from benevolence and goodwill in the face of whatever oppresses you."[14] The remedy to fear, she says, is to accept and embrace it, instead of fighting it. She suggests we try to combat our fears using the weapons of love and kindness. I already felt benevolent toward spiders. I

---

[14] Sylvia Boorstein, "Fear & Fearlessness: What the Buddhists Teach" *Shambhala Sun* (January 2008).

decided that whenever I encountered one I would breathe deeply and think of all the things I liked about them. I would transform my friendly feelings into fearlessness.

* * *

Fears of animals and nature are common and can be deep-seated. Certain animals have physical characteristics that elicit a phobic response in some people. A relative of mine abhors rats because of their naked tails. I have a friend who is frightened of birds. When I asked him why, he shuddered and said, "Beaks and claws." I know a woman who is petrified of bats. Another friend is deeply fearful of being out in the woods at night. She told me this when we were traveling in Japan. Night was falling, and we were wandering through a large wooded compound at a Buddhist temple in Kyoto, trying to find the *shukubo*, or lodging. I had never been afraid of the woods, but I began to feel an upwelling of dread. Fear is contagious, and can be transmitted from one body to another. We were lost on the ancient temple grounds. Pine trees pierced the darkening sky, and as we walked deeper into the labyrinthine compound, I felt trapped in a fairy tale where two children encounter a witch.

Simply knowing a fear is irrational doesn't banish the fear. My bat-phobic friend Julia knows that there is not a single recorded case of a bat ever flying into a person's hair, but it makes not a whit of difference; it has already happened in her imagination. Instead of trying to conquer our fears, a taxing process of struggle and mastery, I prefer Boorstein's notion of trying to find something to love about the things we fear. Throughout human history, the impulse to destroy what we are afraid of has taken a heavy toll on wild creatures of all kinds, from bears and wolves to rattlesnakes and bees. Meeting our fears with loving-kindness—allowing compassion and curiosity to prevail over fear and phobia—may be one of the central tasks of our humanity.

Julia didn't want to hear anything about bats, but I could see her frown wavering when I described the altruistic behavior of vampire bats. These tiny mammals can't go without eating for more than a day or two or they will die. If a bat returns to the roost hungry, the other bats will regurgitate some blood to feed their starving companion. The bat who was helped will later return the favor when needed. Julia was surprised by this account of bat empathy. She was used to thinking of *bats* only in the plural—a swarm of alien creatures just waiting to get entangled in her curly hair. It was the first time she had thought of a bat as an individual, an animal who can feel fear and hunger and maybe even gratitude.

* * *

Sometime during the process of becoming unafraid of spiders, I was driving across the Bay Bridge into San Francisco when a spider descended vertically from the headliner of my car. It stopped just an inch in front of my nose, dangling there as if it was auditioning for a role as a rubber Halloween spider. I sucked in my breath and was about to let out a big satisfying scream, when my rational mind intruded. *You are driving across the bridge!* my rational mind hissed. *Get a grip on yourself!*

I did get a grip. I swallowed the scream and took a couple of deep breaths. I blew the spider away from my face, took hold of the top part of its web with two fingers, and relocated it to the dashboard of my car. I did all this coolly and calmly, as if shuffling giant spiders around at fifty-five miles per hour was something I did every day of my life.

I'm still a long way from spider fearlessness, but just knowing that I have a choice about how to react plants a tiny seed of bravery inside of me. I can sense my fear of spiders retreating like the wraithlike figure in my nightmare, his power evaporating in the face of loving-kindness.

The forest that seems treacherous and shadowy is also a place of beauty and transformation. There in Kyoto, as night fell, a door finally opened, yellow light spilled out, and a young Buddhist monk smiled and beckoned us inside, out of the darkness of the woods. There was nothing to be afraid of, inside or out.

EIGHT

A Small Wild Place

Even as I travel the cities,
I'm more at home in the vacant lots.
—Bob Dylan

I had always been curious about the deer path, a ribbon of hard-packed clay soil that coiled through the neighborhood, bisecting my backyard and many others before vanishing into the foliage at the top of the hillside. One morning, I decided to explore it.

I climbed over the wall and made my way up to the path, which started about 150 feet from my back door. Fallen trees lay across the path in several places, their boughs forming leafy tents. Branches dripped across my face as I ducked under low-hanging limbs. I saw the mouths of burrows tucked under boulders set in the hillside. I nearly tripped over a whitish-gray object protruding from the soil. Thinking it was a shed antler, I knelt for a closer look, brushed the dirt aside, and dug a large bone out of the ground with my knife. Old and desiccated, it could have been the femur bone of a deer. Gently I nudged the bone back into its crevice.

On one side, the path dipped into a gully and crossed an old streambed—Whittle Creek, a tributary of neighboring Sausal Creek. The stream once flowed freely through this canyon, but forty years ago city engineers diverted the creek into an underground culvert, destroying the delicate streamside ecology. Only a vestige of Whittle Creek remained visible on my street: the weir in my next-door neighbor's yard that became a rushing waterway in the rainy season. Tall trees draped in ivy and strangler fig arched over the gully, transforming the urban canyon into a primeval jungle. Though this oasis of land was surrounded by residential streets, and the freeway was only about a mile away, it was so wild and overgrown it was easy to imagine I was in a true wilderness.

As if to contradict that thought, my gaze fell upon a section of rusted metal wrapped around the trunk of an oak tree. It was chicken wire from an old fence that had once separated my property from the property next door. The crude wire fence had long since fallen over and was practically concealed by the ivy and vines that had grown over it. I thought of the spotted fawn I'd seen last week following her mother along the deer path, her dappled coat making her nearly invisible in the shadows. The fawn's tiny hooves were about the same diameter as the holes in the chicken wire. It was just a matter of time before that fawn, or some other animal, stepped on the abandoned fence and became entangled in it.

On the other side, the path veered up the steep hillside. I clambered up the slope, sliding on the ancient layers of leaf duff that had built up over the years to form a thick, slippery surface. I slithered and tripped, clutching at the smooth, ivory trunks of eucalyptus trees as jays screeched a warning at my approach. I was an intruder here. Last year I tried to grow wildflowers on this hillside. I chose a terraced portion of ground halfway up the hill, folded compost into the stony soil, and planted my packet of seeds. Every few days I schlepped a watering can up the hill and sprinkled water on the dry ground, though most of it beaded up and ran off. By spring, only a few seeds had germinated, producing a handful of stunted flowers.

At the summit, I stopped to rest. Looking down, I could see my house, the little green meadow with the white dog standing in it looking up at me curiously. In front of me was a clearing strewn with oaks. Violet shadows flickered in the hazy sunlight. Clouds scudded by. Except for the chirping of birds and the breeze stirring the leaves, it was silent. The field was carpeted with tall golden grass, and here and there were elliptical hollows where the grass was flattened, as if a body had lain down and curled up in each one.

I had found the place where the deer sleep.

This vacant lot at the top of the hill was a small wild place that had remained virtually untouched for years. Deer slept undisturbed and birds nested peacefully. A for-sale sign stuck in the ground was visible from the street on the other side of the lot, but the sign was antique, the phone number nearly indecipherable. Bordered by homes and fences and streets, the field had been left in a natural state for so long it had gone feral. Generations of wild animals had lived in the field, passed through it, grazed, nested, or slept there. For decades, it had been their sanctuary, along with the adjacent hillside that sloped to my house and the deer path they used to negotiate the neighborhood.

The next day I hired a local man with a pickup truck to come tear out the chicken-wire fence and haul it to the landfill. I felt a great sense of satisfaction as I watched him drive away with the rusted fence mounded in the back of his truck.

* * *

That spring, the vacant lot at the top of the hill was purchased by a couple who planned to build their dream home. Since the field was high enough in the foothills to afford a pretty view of the San Francisco Bay, it was a desirable, if somewhat inaccessible home site. The quiet field became a construction zone. Chainsaws came first, followed by bulldozers and other earthmovers. The young oaks at the edges of the property were razed and a steeply curving driveway was graded and covered with blacktop. The sounds of hammers and drills reverberated on the hillside as the timbered skeleton of a three-story house slowly rose from the ground.

One day, I saw a buck making his way down the hillside with what looked like a white bracelet wrapped around his ankle. I grabbed my binoculars. A short length of white plastic pipe, about four or five inches wide, was wedged on the buck's right foreleg. He must have stepped on the scrap of PVC in the construction zone and his hoof went right through it. Now the pipe was stuck, perhaps permanently, on his leg. The buck browsed along the deer path, oblivious to his plastic shackle. His great cupped ears swiveled back and forth as he absorbed each tiny cell of sound around him.

The sight of the plastic pipe stuck on the buck's leg was deeply depressing to me. If it grew too tight it could become infected—and there wasn't a thing I could do about it. It wasn't enough to get rid of one old chicken-wire fence: the city was littered with garbage; with plastic, glass, and metal; with all kinds of menacing objects that could injure and maim and kill. I couldn't protect my wild neighbors from all of that.

So much of our trash winds up in animals' stomachs or stuck on their bodies. When a group of my neighbors cleaned up Sausal Creek one summer they pulled 125 pounds of garbage from the little stream, including forty-four pounds of golf balls. The same month a team of wildlife rescuers in San Jose spent nine days trying to capture a beaver who had a plastic strap—the kind used to bundle newspapers—caught around her midsection. The plastic strap was floating in the Guadalupe River when the beaver swam into it and became ensnared. That beaver was lucky: the rescuers clipped the strap and released the beaver unharmed back into the river.

Urban vacant lots are hardly pristine habitat. Not all of them are as unspoiled as the field at the top of my hillside once was. Still, these neglected weedy fields wedged between houses and buildings are some of the last undeveloped spaces in our communities. Vacant lots, culverts, waysides, and median strips are like tiny wild islands in the city—tough ecosystems that can support entire native plant and animal communities. As they disappear, urban animals have fewer and fewer places to find shelter.

These fragments of land feed our human souls just as they

literally feed wild animals. For some of us, vacant lots are the first variety of wilderness we ever encounter. When I was growing up in Los Angeles, the vacant lot down the street was an enchanted place, a refuge from the smoggy city. In winter the field was covered in thick, green grass. By summer it was seared to a bright gold. I played there every day among the stumps and logs, the heaps of old brick and stone, the forest of jade plants. A thicket of wild oats became a fort. I knew every mysterious hole in the ground where gopher snakes lay silently coiled. That vacant lot has long since been bulldozed and paved over, but it lingers in my memory as it was then, a place so quiet and wild that a girl could rest, in her nest in the tall golden grass.

NINE

The Octopus

hen I was nineteen I got a job working at a pet shop in the San Fernando Valley. It was a small mom-and-pop business tucked into the corner of a strip mall in Reseda, the kind of modest establishment that was common in the days before large corporations took over the business of pets and pet supplies. My job was to care for all the animals, from the fish to the reptiles to the rodents; the shop did not sell dogs or cats.

An alcove in the back of the shop housed a collection of glass tanks containing tropical and saltwater fish. A small octopus lived alone in one tank. With his glistening skin, eight lithe appendages, and bright, watchful eyes, the octopus seemed intensely alien to me. He could squeeze his saclike body into the tiniest crevice, oozing in and out as if he were made of water. When frightened, he would vanish in a haze of ink. At first I was a little put off by his strangeness, but as the weeks went by, that very strangeness began to seem remarkable.

His curiosity was limitless. He would seize any new object placed in his tank and with his eight arms he would methodically explore and touch it all over. Later I learned that octopuses use their suckers both to taste and to touch—each arm is also a kind of tongue—so everything was a multisensory experience for him. He loved to sort through the mound of shells and rocks in his tank, moving them around and rearranging them in little piles. After he became used to me, he would play with my hand, coiling his supple limbs around my fingers, his suction cups gently lapping at my skin. I quickly learned that if the lid of his tank was not securely fastened, the octopus would wriggle out and ooze into a neighboring tank, where he would proceed to dine on the inhabitants or redecorate the tank.

I started looking forward to going to work every day. I was continually thinking up ways to keep the octopus entertained, inventing games or finding objects he could squeeze his body into. I didn't doubt that the being gazing back at me from the other side of the glass had a mind.[15] When I returned to the pet shop after taking a day off, he'd get wildly excited, jetting around his tank and rapidly changing colors, brown to yellow to orange to red—the octopus equivalent of an excited dog jumping up and down.

---

[15] Octopuses can solve complex problems, have short- and long-term memory, and can recognize faces. A 2009 study found that octopuses use tools, such as coconut shells, as shelters or shields. *Scientific American* (Aug. 21, 2012).

My work began to suffer. Instead of sweeping the floor, cleaning cages, or stocking shelves, I could be found stationed at the octopus tank, playing with my new friend or pretending to wipe down the glass. Sometimes I would just stand there watching as he hung suspended in the water, inflating and deflating like a balloon, or oozing into his rocky den for a nap. I lived in fear that someone would buy him. On my minimum-wage salary I could not afford to set up a saltwater aquarium at home. When a customer showed interest in the octopus, our conversation would go something like this:

"What can you tell me about that little brown octopus over there?"

"Um, that's a pretty boring animal, hides under a rock all the time. A very picky eater. I don't recommend it. How about one of these nice angelfish instead?"

One day, the owner of the shop overheard me talking a customer out of buying the octopus. She took me aside and told me, not unkindly, that she didn't think working at the pet shop was a "good fit" for me. She let me go that day.

At home, disgraced, I pined for the octopus. I worried he would think I had abandoned him and he would languish in his tank. I was sure no one would care for him the way I had. My friend Eva could not understand my attachment to a creature she regarded as an insensate fish. "How can you love an animal that can't love you back?" she asked.

I was pretty sure the octopus *did* love me back, but I told Eva it didn't matter whether he did or not, and to my surprise, this was true. The love I felt for this little marine animal wasn't linear, but multidirectional, flowing around us like an ocean of seawater. As I had fed the octopus, played with and protected him, I had come to understand him, and in understanding him, I had come to love him.

I'd met several customers who were devoted to their unusual pets. I knew a man who doted on his tarantula; a couple who rarely went on vacation because they hated to leave their tortoise home alone; a woman whose pet iguana slept in a heated dog bed at the foot of her bed. Our desire to form emotional bonds with others is so strong that almost any animal can be lovable, if our hearts are open to it. Love may have a hard shell or quivering whiskers. It may slither or crawl. Or it may have four pairs of arms and a beaky mouth.

I finally worked up the courage to return to the pet shop for a visit. When the octopus spied me walking down the aisle toward his tank, he rose to the surface and greeted me with a vibrant display of changing colors. The next time I visited, his tank was empty.

Though the octopus and I lived in different worlds, his watery and weightless, mine solid and accountable to gravity, we were connected by a filament of understanding. I remember how I used to place the tip of my finger on the outside of his tank. He would press his arm against the same spot, as if he was trying to get as close to me as possible despite the glass that separated us. It was our ritual: two species, each alone, yet together.

TEN

Golden Season

hen winter's tall grass turns bright gold and shimmers in the heat, when the oaks are so dry their rustling leaves make music in the wind, it's golden season in California. Native plants know how to survive the dry season, while the exotics weaken and wither for lack of moisture. Goldfinches feast on dried seedheads and a lone blue dragonfly skims the last trickle of water in a puddle. The air smells like chaparral, and as an afternoon breeze stirs the trees I hear the golden music of summer.

Golden season coincides with fire season. Every year the city and many private landowners hire goats to eat brush and shrubs that pose a fire danger. Driving through the foothills I often see large herds of goats contained by orange portable fences, browsing on the hillsides. The next time I drive by, the goats are gone and the landscape is stripped of vegetation.

* * *

One morning I was in my garden when I heard a peculiar sound, a sound I was sure I had never heard before. Loud and abrupt, the sound was somewhere between a bleat, a moan, and a yelp. *Blee-ee-ah-elp!* I got my binoculars and scanned the hillside. Nothing. Perhaps it was a baby in one of the neighboring houses. A few minutes later I heard the sound again. *Blee-ee-ah-elp!* Now I was sure something was seriously amiss. I searched the hillside again. There in the viewfinder, near the top of the hill, I saw the head of some exotic animal, twisting and turning, its horns going this way and that. It was a goat, I realized, and it was trapped.

"Michael, come out here and look at this," I called. My husband was used to being summoned outside to see a new species of bird, a deer with a fawn, or the wild turkeys promenading through our backyard. I handed him the binoculars.

"Is that what I think it is?" he said.

The next time I looked, I noticed a man on a deck above the goat, talking on a cell phone. The goat continued to make its unnerving sounds, the sound of an animal in extremis, but the man seemed unconcerned. Something was wrong here. This goat was in trouble.

"Maybe he's planning to kill the goat," I said. "Maybe he's going to slaughter it and barbecue it on Sunday. He's on the phone now inviting all his relatives." That was it: the man was fattening up the goat, and he didn't care that it was stuck because he was just going to butcher it in a few hours. "We have to save that goat," I said.

The hill on that side was high and steep and densely planted, impossible to scale on foot. We got in our car, though we had no idea where the goat actually was. The property belonged to someone who lived above us, but we didn't know which house. We drove along the winding roads that traversed the neighborhood with the windows rolled down, listening for the telltale sound of a distraught goat.

* * *

When I was a kid I used to love watching the TV game show, "Let's Make a Deal." I could never understand why the contestants acted so disappointed when they picked the door with a llama or a goat behind it. What kind of person would want bedroom furniture or kitchen appliances when she could have her own goat? I spent my childhood with three goats, Polly, Tish and Nanny, who lived at my elementary school in Echo Park, a stone's throw from downtown Los Angeles. The school principal, Miss Mason, thought it was important for city kids to have animals in their lives. She had created a small urban farm at Elysian Heights Elementary that included a garden and a barnyard with the goats, a sheep, a Shetland pony, a small flock of chickens, and some ducks. All of us sixth-graders got to take turns helping in the barnyard, mucking straw, collecting eggs, grooming the pony, and learning how to care for the animals.

In a photograph taken of our sixth-grade class, I am

standing next to Miss Mason, who wears a sleeveless black-and-white sheath embellished with a pattern of orange butterflies. The sun glints off her coppery red hair. Miss Mason insisted on including the animals in our class portraits, so Polly the goat is just in front of me. Her little black and white face looks out of the past, one of her ears grazing the cheek of a boy on her other side. I remember this day well because Polly kept untucking my shirt with her mobile, rubbery upper lip, nibbling at the fabric while I swatted her away with one hand.

At the time, I was intimidated by Miss Mason—she was so tall, strict, and formidable—but in hindsight I can see what a remarkable woman she was, both shrewd and compassionate. About a decade before I was born, a skinny alley cat had jumped through an open window into a classroom. The gray tabby was given the name Room 8, and Miss Mason gave him sanctuary at Elysian Heights for the rest of his life. By the time I started kindergarten, Room 8 was a very old cat, and so fat the school janitor had to lift him onto the windowsill so he could nap in the sun. On the first day of school every September, Miss Mason would carry Room 8 from class to class, introducing him to all the new students and instructing everyone to be kind and gentle to him. Her cardinal rule was *Don't disturb the cat*.

* * *

Rounding another corner, Michael and I strained to hear the sounds of bleating.

"Do you hear it?" he asked.

"I think so," I said. "Wait—yes! This has to be it, right here."

We parked the car and walked down a short flight of steps on the side of a house. A man was standing on a patio at the bottom of the steps, staring at his cell phone. Behind him I saw the goat.

"We live below you and we heard your goat crying for help," I said. No reason not to come right out with it. If this guy was a potential goat killer I didn't want to get too friendly with him. In a more neighborly tone, Michael asked, "Do you need some help?"

"He's got his head stuck in the fence again," the man said, gesturing wildly at the goat. "This is the second time! The goatherd won't answer his phone. I don't know what to do."

When he saw our puzzled expressions, he explained that he had hired five goats to clear the brush around his house. The goatherd had dropped the goats off early this morning and said he'd be back to get them later that day. In the meantime, one goat was stuck in the fence, and another goat had wandered several streets away and was on the lam. Chaos reigned.

He was not a goat killer. He was just an ordinary guy with a goat problem.

"We can help you get him out," Michael said. The man was reluctant to cut the portable fence the goatherd had erected—"What if I have to pay for it?" he grumbled—but we persuaded him it was the right thing to do. Michael got a pair of wirecutters out of the car, and as I consoled the goat, he snipped a few wires and the goat was free.

The goat, who was the color of salt and pepper and had a pointed little gray beard (a goatee, in fact) shook his head vigorously. He eyed a rose bush on the other side of the fence. He stretched out his neck and stuck his head through the fence to grab a mouthful of rose petals. When the goat tried to pull his head back, his backward-arching horns snagged on the wire. He twisted his head to the side and looked at us sadly with his amber eyes. *Blee-ee-ah-elp!* We all jumped.

"Aren't goats supposed to be smart?" Michael said.

"You see, there he goes again!" said the man, exasperated. "No matter how many times I get him out, he just does it again!"

* * *

There was another reason I liked "Let's Make a Deal." I was riveted by the idea that you could choose your own future. Choice was terrifying and powerful, random and arbitrary. If you chose well, you were lucky. If you chose poorly? Too bad. Room 8's life illustrated the phenomenon of dumb luck: it wasn't fate but a fluke that he jumped into the right classroom. If he had jumped into Room 6, things might have turned out differently—the teacher might have thrust the cat back into his life of deprivation and hunger. This proved to me how random things were.

These are the kinds of reflections that come to me in golden season. I look at that sixth-grade photograph and our young faces look back, open and wondering. Polly the goat and I wear twinned expressions of puzzlement. The two of us were not so different then, in the way that children and animals have an affinity, a bond forged by their innocence and inexperience, their vulnerability and lack of agency. It wasn't long before our paths would diverge—I would grow up and go out into the world to make my own choices while Polly would stay behind in the barnyard; she would never grow up.

Decades later I returned to Echo Park and walked across the blacktop playground of the elementary school to the barnyard. Some kids were playing kickball on the playground and their shouts echoed in my ears. The large pen that used to be full of animals munching hay or dozing in the sunshine was empty. The roof of the little goat shed was falling in, the chicken coop deserted. The garden was overgrown with weeds.

I stared through the chain-link fence at the old wooden trough, remembering all the times I had filled it with flakes of sweet-smelling alfalfa as the sheep and the three goats eagerly jostled each other aside. I remembered waking up at home in the muffled darkness of early morning to the crowing of the school rooster. I remembered Miss Mason clicking into my classroom on her sensible pumps and standing before us with her perfect posture and her cranberry-colored lips. Room 8 had died by then, at the age of twenty-two, and his obituary had appeared in the *Los Angeles Times*. He had become a world-famous cat, the subject of television newscasts, magazine articles, even a children's book. Miss Mason looked around the room, making eye contact with each child, and in her gravelly smoker's voice, she said, "Boys and girls, always be kind to animals, and they will repay your kindness someday." That's the deal she struck with us. All these years later, it's still the best deal I've ever made.

ELEVEN

The Outsiders

He recognized the wistful melody of the plaintive
little mew, the cry of the waif, the stray,
the unloved, and the homeless.
— Paul Gallico

Not long after Michael and I moved into our Oakland house, I spied a phantom lurking on the hillside. The colors of shadow and chaparral, the elusive creature blended effortlessly into the background. As the phantom slunk behind a tree and then materialized again, I saw that it was a cat, tawny beige with black stripes on its legs and tail, with a pair of bright blue eyes that watched me with suspicion and fear.

I began putting out bowls of tuna. At first the cat would run the instant it saw me, but gradually, lured by the tantalizing scent, it began to creep closer. One triumphant day after I'd gone inside the house, the cat ventured down off the hillside to eat, devouring the tuna while casting anxious glances around, as if afraid someone was going to come and snatch the food away at any moment.

Looking through the window I was able to observe the cat more closely. I saw that her ear was notched, which told me that at some point in her past, she'd been trapped, spayed, and vaccinated for rabies. Then someone had released her back into the only home she'd ever known—the dead-end street where I live and its adjacent hillside. This process is known by the acronym TNR, for trap-neuter-return, and it's widely considered to be the most compassionate and practical way to manage feral cats, or community cats, as they are also called. A TNR program can stabilize and gradually reduce the population of cats (though it works only if cat owners also sterilize their roaming pets). Perhaps the same kindly stranger who had this cat spayed had fed her for a while, but moved away or died, or maybe the cat was so timid that more dominant cats had driven her away from the feeding station. That's a part of her story I'll never know.

I've seen community cats in every country I've ever visited, in every state and every city. There are now as many free-roaming cats in the United States as there are owned cats, which is to say tens of millions of cats living in the shadows of our society.[16] They creep around the edges of hotels and apartment buildings; they live below freeway overpasses and on the edges of bus- and train-station parking lots; in city parks, at cemeteries, and on college campuses. There is a lot of dispute about the numbers of birds and wildlife these cats kill, and

---

[16] The Humane Society of the United States estimates that there are 50 million feral cats in the United States.

controversy about the way such studies are conducted, but nearly everyone agrees that the cats have a somewhat adverse effect on birds, lizards, and small mammal species.

* * *

On a trip to Maui, Michael and I went hiking in the lush Iao Valley. Two days later we returned to the valley, not to hike, but because neither of us could forget the cats we'd seen living in the jungle on the edges of the parking lot, subsisting on scraps from visitors, lizards, insects, and many of Maui's increasingly endangered forest birds. Many of these cats had been born here and were completely wild, while others were former pets who had been dumped to fend for themselves.

One cat in particular stayed lodged in my mind: an under-sized, homely fellow who looked, as my father used to say, as if he were made of all the spare parts left over after God finished making cats. Spotted, striped, and splotched; bowlegged, rheumy eyed, and tatter-eared; Little Iao, as I called him, was inseparable from his friend, a dark gray tabby. Little Iao must have once had a home because he seemed to yearn for human contact. He rubbed his body against my legs, and I stroked his head while his anxious tabby friend watched from a distance.

* * *

Unlike other domesticated animals, cats never completely lost their ability to survive in the wild; yet unlike true wild animals, feral cats are drawn to people, often living near human habitations. They live on the fringes, always the outsiders. A feral cat's best hope is to find a human caretaker, someone who will have the cat sterilized and then provide regular food for the duration of its life.[17] Caring for feral cats is a stewardship, as these cats truly belong to the communities in which they live. Feral cats exist because of us, so they belong to all of us. They are a part of the commons. Without any human help, their circumstances are often wretched, and their lives difficult and short.

One summer I happened upon a feral cat colony in the Sacramento River Delta. The cats were living inside a giant blackberry bramble, a tangled warren of passageways and burrows across the street from a tributary of the river. These cats had not yet been trapped and sterilized (though they would be later that summer), and one of the females had a litter of just-weaned kittens. I peeked into one burrow and was shocked to see the picked-over carcass of a red-tailed hawk. A cat could never kill a raptor of that size—the bird was most likely hit by a car on the roadway and then dragged here by the mother cat. I pictured the desperate cat tugging the dead hawk by its wing a quarter mile along the road, down the grassy ditch, and into the bramble where her litter of ravenous kittens awaited.

* * *

At the end of my street there's a private school campus with open land and trees that has become a dumping ground for unwanted cats. My neighbor, Barbara, does TNR for the feral

---

17   Alley Cat Allies: alleycat.org

cats in our neighborhood. She has single-handedly been trapping, sterilizing, and feeding these cats for years. Her tidy, airy house is cat HQ: there are cat toys, beds, bowls, and litter boxes indoors and out. She has six pet cats of her own and she feeds at least twelve outdoor community cats.

Visiting Barbara's house one morning, I caught glimpses of cats everywhere: on the deck, hiding in the shrubbery, vanishing into the grove of eucalyptus trees that borders the school campus. With Barbara's care, regular meals, and a safe place to live on her property, these ferals would live out their lives as "garden cats," healthy and content. Barbara told me there was only one cat she hadn't yet captured, a wily old tomcat who had figured out how to elude her traps. She smiled. "But I'll get him. Just wait and see."

Some people in the neighborhood call Barbara a crazy cat lady—she even good-humoredly calls herself that—but there is nothing crazy about Barbara or the work she does. She is one of the sanest and most compassionate people I know. She has devoted her life to caring for these forgotten cats, these exiles. Without Barbara, the population of cats in our neighborhood would explode. That would mean more starving kittens and desperate young mothers, more stress on birds and lizards, and more aggravation for humans who don't relish the sounds of caterwauling at night.

* * *

In Maui, Michael and I had brought a case of cat food with us when we returned to the parking lot in the Iao Valley. Maybe one meal wouldn't make much of a difference in their lives, but it would make a difference today, we reasoned. As we scooped the food onto leaves and placed the leaves under shrubs to protect them from the steadily falling rain, dozens of hungry cats materialized from the edges of the forest. We watched the cats eat until we started to get soaked through, and then we got in our car to leave. I saw Little Iao slip under the guardrail to drink from a puddle. He looked so small and woeful crouched in the rain, his sodden fur plastered down along his back. We drove out of the parking lot and turned onto the road that leads back down to the main highway. When I turned back for one last look, Little Iao was gone.

As for the blue-eyed phantom on my hillside, today she eats two meals a day and when it's cold and rainy, she sleeps in a warm, dry shelter under the eaves of our house. Michael has named her Gumdrop. I remember the first time I heard her purr; she looked surprised, as if she didn't know she was capable of producing this steady hum of well-being. She still runs away when other people or cats come near, but she's taken the bold step of allowing me to touch her, and she seems to know her hungry days are behind her. As wary and wild as Gumdrop is, caring for her is deeply rewarding. She is the perennial outsider, the blameless outcast. When I bring her in out of the shadows, I also come home to myself.

TWELVE

The Patch Table

In my early twenties I spent a summer in Ketchikan, Alaska, working in a salmon cannery. My job was to stand at a section of conveyer belt called the patch table. I held a large pair of curved scissors and grabbed can after can off the conveyer belt trimming the bits of white bone and translucent salmon flesh that spilled over the lip of the can. Grab and trim, grab and trim, up to fourteen hours a day, six or seven days a week, as long as the salmon run lasted.

Standing with me at the patch table were Tlingit Indian women who worked with rapid, experienced movements. Their ancestors had been fishing for salmon in the waters of southeastern Alaska for thousands of years. Their totem poles, carved with eagles, bears, and ravens, still stood guardian around the island. I had climbed Deer Mountain and found a totem at the peak, a slender cedar pole carved with a winged beaver facing west, toward the open ocean.

Most of these women ignored the young seasonal workers like me, who arrived on the ferry in June for a summer of work and adventure, and departed at the end of the season. But Dora was younger than the others, about my age, and she was curious and friendly. Dora had never been outside the Alaskan panhandle and no one in her family had traveled further than Sitka. She thought it was hilarious that I had come to Alaska all the way from California. What was California like, she wanted to know. When I told her she should go see it for herself, she just laughed. Dora's sense of self was so deeply rooted in this place that she could not imagine living anywhere else. She was Dora because she lived here among her people, who had made her who and what she was.

Unlike Dora, I had no ancestral home and my identity was not entwined with any particular place. My grandparents had come to America from a handful of Eastern European countries I had never visited. They were buried among strangers in graveyards far from their homes. Neither of my parents had remained in the cities of their birth, and neither had I for very long. There was much I couldn't know about the unfolding mystery of my life. But there was one thing I could count on: the unknown city I visited one year might be my home the next.

* * *

Every morning I entered the cannery through the great wooden doors and punched the time clock. I walked drowsing the mile home at night and I walked drowsing the mile back the next morning. I saw the dorsal fins of pilot whales skimming the glassy surface of Tongass Narrows. I saw bald eagles perched on the pilings sunk in the shallow waters. I saw black bears foraging at the Ketchikan city dump. On the back dock of the cannery sat enormous metal tubs of dead salmon, their bodies glistening with rain. I had seen salmon struggling upstream in the creek that ran through town. From the bridge next to the Ketchikan public library I had watched the fish hurling their bodies at the rocks until the water tumbling over the dam foamed pink with blood.

No matter what our backgrounds, all of the workers at the cannery were united by our mutual exhaustion. We stole sleep on our lunch hours, on dinner breaks, in the precious moments compressed between whistle blasts. I'd climb the ladder into the warehouse attic, where old seiner nets were cast about in loose mounds. The nets smelled briny but they were warm and dry. When I awoke I'd find other workers slumbering in the nets, ensnared in the strands of twine like sea creatures brought up from the deep.

Even my waking hours were spent in a kind of half sleep. I watched the river of cans flow by, headed for the press where the lids would be sealed on before going into the steamer. One day when I was working at the patch table, another seasonal worker named Andrew discovered a live salmon among the tubs of dead fish that had just been wheeled in from the dock. It seemed impossible, but this fish had survived being netted in the ocean, dumped into the hold of the seiner, and delivered to the dock. Andrew paraded the miracle fish around the cannery, holding it over his head as it gasped for breath, its mouth slowly opening and closing. The Tlingits watched the spectacle impassively.

Even though I was part of the assembly line whose job it was to stuff virtual rivers of salmon into cans, this single salmon's life suddenly seemed precious to me and I couldn't bear to see it suffer. I begged Andrew to take the salmon to the dock outside the factory doors. He called me a spoilsport, but he complied.

Outside, I watched Andrew toss the fish into the Narrows. It sank beneath the surface, falling deeper and deeper through the green water until we lost sight of it. I went back inside, trying to ignore the foreman scowling at me from his perch on his metal stool. Dora was standing next to me at the patch table. She gave me an odd look. This was another area where we had trouble understanding each other—what she saw as my sentimentality toward animals. She had smiled politely when I showed her a photograph of my dog, who was being cared for by a friend back in California. In the photo my arms were around him as we curled together on the couch.

It was difficult to talk at the patch table because the noise from the machinery was so loud. I bent to my work. Grab and trim, grab and trim. I mentally reviewed the Tlingit words Dora had taught me. While she wasn't fluent in her native tongue, she knew the words for the animals on the totem poles: *ch'áak'* was eagle, *kéet* was the orca, *yéil* was the raven, and *xáat* was the salmon.

To pass the long, monotonous hours I tried to remember everything that had ever happened to me. I unraveled my life

backward: And then? And then? I asked myself, as if I were
story and storyteller both. Through my reverie I heard the
Tlingit women murmuring to each other. Dora had told me
there was no word in Tlingit for "I" and like a sleepwalker
abruptly awakened I understood that their stories were about
a world vast beyond my imagining, while my story was only
about myself.

* * *

At the end of July I said goodbye to Dora.

"See you next summer," we said, the standard farewell,
although I had no idea if I would ever return to Ketchikan.

It's a quirk of human nature that we generally care more
about the one than we do about the many. Our imaginations
are captured by stories, and those stories always feature individuals. When I look back upon that exhausting, extraordinary summer, the one image that always rises painfully to
mind is that salmon, gasping for oxygen in Andrew's arms. I
didn't spare a thought for the multitudes of fish going into the
cans, each of whom had suffered identically. That lone
salmon, singled out from the masses, was the only one that
had mattered, the only one that became real to me. I saved
one life while millions of others perished. That doesn't make
me any kind of hero; I suppose it makes me human.

THIRTEEN

Only a Goldfish

Two goldfish used to live outdoors on my patio in a ceramic basin filled with aquatic plants. I had purchased the two fish from an aquarium in Chinatown, where they were crammed in a tank with at least a hundred other "feeder" goldfish. Floating near the top of the tank was a dead goldfish. Like most fish, goldfish have a keen sense of smell so they were aware of the fish decomposing in their tank and they were doing their best to avoid it. When I pointed out the dead fish to the proprietor, he said he'd remove it later.

"How about now?" I asked, as he did not seem overly busy. "Could you please do it now?"

He shrugged and netted the fish, and tossed it in the wastebasket.

* * *

The unfortunate goldfish ranks as the most disposable creature on earth. Many a joke is made of the goldfish's fleeting
lifespan and its propensity for being flushed down toilets. In
reality, goldfish do not have short lifespans: properly cared for,
in a suitable tank with good water quality, a goldfish can easily
live for ten to fifteen years and beyond. The oldest known
goldfish, Tish, was forty-three when he finally expired in
1999, breaking the previous record-holder's age of forty-one.
Originally bright orange, Tish turned pure silver in his old
age. "I don't think we will be getting another one. We
couldn't replace Tish; he was part of the family," said his
bereaved owner, whose son had won the fish at a carnival in
Yorkshire in 1956.[18]

I named my two goldfish Lucky and Spot. Lucky was
larger than Spot and entirely orange, so it was easy to tell
them apart. The water in their new home was cold, the way
goldfish like it, and they could swim in a circle without
bumping into a transparent glass wall. They had plenty of
plants to hide in and nibble on. A golden bamboo growing in
a tub on the patio provided abundant shade.

One day I kneeled by the bowl and looked in, but didn't
see either fish. This was not unusual: the water was murky,
the ceramic bowl was opaque, and Spot and Lucky often
napped near the bottom of the bowl, dreaming their goldfish
dreams. I got up to leave when I heard something rustling in
the bamboo leaves on the ground next to the bowl. I looked

---

[18]   BBC News: news.bbc.co.uk/2/hi/uk/414114.stm

down and there on the concrete patio was Lucky, his orange body encrusted in dirt, one red-rimmed eye staring up at me in desperation. People who say that fish have no expressions are simply wrong.

He must have summoned the last of his strength to flap his tail and attract my attention. I took all this in in the instant it took me to grab Lucky and plunge him back into the water. Spot instantly emerged from wherever she had been hiding and swam up to Lucky, bumping him with her nose. As he floated, inert, she bumped him again and again. I held my breath. Finally, Lucky began to swim slowly forward, and within a few minutes he had completely recovered from his ordeal.

* * *

I'd had the idea to create this outdoor water garden quite some time ago. I had researched fish and read up on pond biology. I'd looked at many types of containers before buying what I thought was the perfect large ceramic basin. The basin sat empty on the patio for a year until I finally got around to getting the aquatic plants, establishing them in the bowl, and adding the two fish. I was thrilled with the result—it was a serene, balanced ecosystem that gave me a feeling of tranquility whenever I looked at it. But this episode had made me nervous. I hadn't reckoned on a fish being so adventurous.

A couple of weeks later, during a heavy rainstorm, my cat Puck burst in the cat door in great excitement, meowing in a curious muffled manner, until I realized he was holding something in his mouth. It was Lucky! The rain had raised the water level in the basin to the rim and Lucky must have slid right out and onto the patio where Puck discovered him. (At least, that was how I reconstructed the crime scene, giving the cat the benefit of the doubt.) I grabbed the little fish and sprinted to the bowl. This time, I was sure I had lost him—he had been inside a cat's mouth—but a few moments after putting him back in the water he was swimming around as if it was any other ordinary day.

I, however, was a nervous wreck. The tranquil feelings I associated with my water garden had evaporated. Because of the taller plants growing in the basin, I couldn't place a net over the top. I worried about Lucky constantly whenever I was away from home, and when I was home, I checked on him every hour. Most of the time I found him swimming placidly around the bowl, with Spot by his side. But I was sure it was only a matter of time before he fell out again, or was plucked from the bowl, or started breeching like a whale and landed on the street in front of the house—and next time I might not be around to save him. I started searching for a new home for the two fish.

I had a new appreciation for goldfish after my year with Lucky and Spot. My little fish were individuals with distinct personalities: Lucky clearly felt the need to experience terra firma while Spot never showed the slightest inclination for exploring the world outside her bowl. At the same time, they were bonded to each other. Fish are schooling animals who become anxious when they're alone. It always pains me to see a goldfish living in one of those tiny spherical bowls, with no companion, room to swim, or plants to hide in. They may be called goldfish bowls, but no goldfish ever survives for very long in one of them.[19]

* * *

Recently I saw two beautiful fancy goldfish living in a small bowl on the counter of a hotel lobby in San Francisco. The fish were much too big for the bowl and they hovered near the top, gasping for air from the surface of the water. They did this because they were asphyxiating in the tiny bowl, which could not generate enough oxygen in the water to support the two fish. When I suggested to the manager that the fish would live longer, happier lives if they were moved to a larger tank, he explained to me that the hotel chain had a policy requiring each of its hotels to display a pair of goldfish in a bowl of this size and shape—no larger, no smaller—on the reception counter.

The hotel must have gone through many goldfish. When the fish died, they simply purchased new fish, since goldfish were so inexpensive. The fish were merely part of the décor; their lives were worthless. As I tried to think of something to say to change the manager's mind, an older woman who had been waiting in the lobby stepped up to the desk. I was sure she was going to complain about the wait. Instead, she said, "You just let the fish die instead of getting them a proper tank."

"Well," the manager said. "They're only goldfish, and—"

---

[19] Several municipalities, including Rome, Italy, have banned the sale of these small spherical bowls for depriving fish of oxygen.

"That's appalling," she said.

"Yeah," said a guy who had been rapidly swiping away on his phone while he waited his turn to check in. "Why can't you just change your policy? This is the twenty-first century, after all."

There were four or five other people in the lobby, and they were all listening attentively to this exchange.

"Yes. That would be a nice thing to do for the fish," said a young woman with curly black hair who was holding the hand of a little girl. "Don't you think so, Izzy?"

The little girl nodded. "We have fish at home," she said imperiously. "They wouldn't like being squashed in that little bowl." She looked up at the manager. "It's mean."

The manager looked embarrassed. "I suppose, um, I could see about getting the policy changed. It's probably outdated," he conceded.

I gave him a grateful smile and he smiled back. I'm always amazed to find compassion in the unlikeliest of places. Most people, given the chance, really do care about animals and they want to do the right thing—even if it's only a goldfish.

I finally relocated Lucky and Spot to a neighborhood nursery, where they shared a roomy, galvanized-steel horse trough with a half dozen other goldfish. The fish were not for sale, and they had aquatic plants to hide in and plenty of shade. It was goldfish nirvana. When I visited the nursery to buy plants I would always stop by the horse trough to check on them. No one believed me, but even long after Spot's black spots had faded to orange and Lucky had doubled in size, I could still recognize my two goldfish, swimming side by side.

FOURTEEN

Wild Gardeners

Nature is a chain of dominoes:
if you pull one piece out, the whole thing falls down.
—Caroline Fraser

A squirrel has been following me around the backyard, watching me garden. Actually, she *escorts* me around the backyard. Rufus, as I call her, has been here a lot longer than I have, and she knows the lay of the land. She is a bold squirrel, not above tapping at the backdoor to request a walnut. She's frugal: she buries two out of every four nuts. I watch her dig a hole; it's always the perfect size. She places the nut in the hole, brushes the soft soil back in around the hole, then gently but firmly tamps it down with her little hands splayed flat. Then she turns and looks at me, sits back on her heels, and crosses her furry arms. *Did you get all that?*

Say what you will about squirrels; they are tireless. Rufus is constantly on the move, collecting nuts, burying nuts, checking on the location of previously buried nuts, and debating the merits of nuts with other squirrels. Whenever I look out the window I see Rufus, or one of her extended family members, leaping, scampering, or scurrying somewhere in a great hurry. I have never seen Rufus sleep, or even lean up against a tree and take a breather. I know Rufus is an early riser because every morning at daybreak I am awakened by the drumbeat of little squirrel feet scuttling across my rooftop. To a squirrel, my house is simply a peculiar four-sided tree with a flat crown and no leaves that provides a convenient bridge when traveling through the treetops.

Like all squirrels, Rufus is a hoarder. Her nuts and seeds are buried in secret caches for dining on over the winter or whenever she wants a convenient snack. Squirrels may bury thousands of nuts in hundreds of different locations—this is called scatter hoarding. But since they can't remember the exact location of every single cache, some of those prudently buried nuts and seeds germinate and become trees. In this way, squirrels, who are found on every continent except Antarctica, have planted a large percentage of the planet's forests. Many a black walnut, hazelnut, beechnut, or pinenut that was stored in the ground and later forgotten has become a tree. After fires have destroyed large swathes of forests, squirrels help replant by bringing seeds to burned areas and pushing them into the soil.

We have the squirrels, and several species of blue jays, to thank for much of the vast oak woodlands throughout North America. Acorns are relatively large seeds, too heavy to be scattered by the wind. Without animals to transport them to other places, acorns would not get much farther than gravity can take them as they fall from the tree and roll down the hill, if the tree is lucky enough to be on a slope.

Judging by the thrum of activity on my roof, I think the jays are storing acorns in the rain gutter, which is full of oak and eucalyptus debris, a perfect hiding place. The fact that jays and squirrels cache food shows that while they may live in the present, they are aware of the future and they actively plan for it. Experience—and maybe their mothers—has taught them that the future means *a time in which I may be hungry*.

Many gardeners I know regard squirrels as a nuisance since they raid bird feeders and dig up freshly planted flower beds. My neighbor Ben was frustrated when a squirrel kept digging up the pumpkin seeds he'd planted in his raised bed. Then he came across a pumpkin vine growing on its own in a sunny corner of the backyard. He left the rogue vine alone and watched it grow into a mammoth vine that yielded enormous pumpkins. He had to admit the squirrel was a better gardener than he was.

Back in my vegetable-gardening days, I tended to divide animals into two groups: a creature was either beneficial to me (and my squash/lettuce/chard), or it was harmful. Now these categories seemed narrow and arbitrary. Many creatures that ended up in my "harmful" column play critical roles in the environment. The ever-exasperating mosquito is a significant source of protein for the hummingbird, which is an important pollinator. Hummingbirds also consume aphids, gnats, mites, and fruit flies, none of which I'm very fond of. If all of these vexing insects disappeared, so would the hummingbird.

While it sometimes gives me the creeps thinking of all the spiders that populate my garden, not only do birds like to eat spiders, many birds use spider silk to bind their nests to branches. Without spiders, the nests would fall out of trees more easily, crushing the eggs or killing the nestlings.

Ants stage an annual assault on my house and create quite a nuisance. Yet ants are some of the most important animals among us. Ants are the planet's housekeepers and the original practitioners of reduce-recycle-reuse. The ten million billion ants in the world are always constantly hard at work, carrying away dead insects and rotting carcasses to their nests, removing food debris, tilling the soil, pollinating plants, and dispersing seeds. During a visit to Costa Rica several years ago I met a naturalist who showed me long columns of leafcutter ants, each carrying a fragment of leaf on its back. They carry the leaves back to their nests, where they use them to cultivate an edible fungus. These ants can defoliate an entire tree in a day. Without the leafcutters, the naturalist told me, no sunlight would penetrate the rainforest and the canopy would grow too thick for new, younger plants to flourish.

My friend Mark joined the Peace Corps after college and spent two years in the Marshall Islands. In one of his letters to me, Mark wrote that he had to keep his hut very neat: clothes had to be folded or hung up, shoes lined up in a row, bed made. The reason for this uncharacteristic tidiness was, if he threw his things all over the floor, as was his wont, it would attract ants. He said the ants on the island of Majuro had some kind of supernatural ability to detect disarray. Disarray implies chaos, chaos indicates rot, and rot—to an ant—generally means food.

The ants of disorder changed Mark temporarily from a slob into a neatnik.

In the urban wilds of zooburbia, I am learning to be more observant. I see that animals and plants shape our lives and each other's lives in ways both subtle and profound. Every being has a place on earth and a job to do. Elephants, badgers, peacocks, dragonflies, starfish, squirrels, ants, apples and elm trees, turquoise and amethyst, bacteria and microorganisms; all are essential, none are disposable.

Rufus continues to teach me how to garden. She is also teaching me to plan for the future, not by obsessing over it, but by being prepared, stashing a few nuts here and there. I feel like such an amateur. But I'm learning. I just have to watch the squirrel.

FIFTEEN

Gravity

But this blue I'm compelled to glorify
it's not robin's egg, navy, or indigo;
it's a shade that should be named "devastation blue."
—Claire Bateman

There's a mysterious staircase in my backyard. It winds sinuously up the hill, bordered on each side by a rock retaining wall, and then ends, abruptly, in the middle of the hillside. There's nothing at the top of the stairs—nothing at all. The last owner of this house built the staircase, hacking each step out of the stony soil and stacking rocks on either side to make the wall. Possibly he never had time to complete it. He left his pickaxe embedded in the soil at the top of the last step, as if he had just stopped for a break and intended to come back and take up where he left off. The pickaxe is gradually being buried by the soil and rocks that constantly drift down the hill. Gravity brings everything downhill, eventually. I have found all kinds of odd objects sitting at the bottom of the hill: the wooden caboose from a toy train set, marbles, an old glass jar stamped "Alhambra Distilled Water," a rusted pail, a spark plug.

One afternoon I watched a feather fall from the sky. It glided through the canopy of oaks, fell headlong down the stairway, and came to rest on the surface of the meadow. I picked up the feather and turned it over, admiring the shimmering bands of blue—indigo, sapphire, and cobalt. It was the feather of a Steller's blue jay. I held the feather up to the sun and the blue turned a drab gray. The blue of a jay's feather is not really blue at all; it's a trick of the light, created when the light enters the feather.

I aimed my binoculars up the hill, and high above the unfinished staircase I spotted a Steller's jay sitting in the dirt, just sitting there. Her uncharacteristic stillness alarmed me. Steller's jays are active, boisterous birds, always in motion, busy and bossy. I watched the jay, waiting for her to fly away. When she finally made her move, it was immediately apparent that she could not fly. She got to her feet, hopped forward, then tumbled head over heels. She slid a few feet down the hill before she regained her balance. She made another hop and slid again. The bird seemed determined to get down the hill. I watched her agonizing descent, wondering where she was going. Finally the crippled jay made it to the bottom of the hill and flopped over the wall down onto the flat meadow in my backyard. She rested there a few moments, and then she hopped up onto the rim of the birdbath and took a long, deep, drink of water.

The birdbath had been her destination all along. That's why she sat still for so long at the top of the hill: she was mapping out her route so she would land in the right place. The thirsty jay drank for a long time, perched on the rim of the birdbath, gulping water. And then, despite myself, I thought of Big Gray.

* * *

Big Gray was a very wild feral cat who once lived in the neighborhood. One day he disappeared, as ferals tend to do. I helped my neighbor Jan look for him—she had been feeding him and his brother for several years and was worried when he disappeared—but we couldn't find him anywhere. A week later, I was walking up my front steps when I heard a rustle in the shrubbery. It was Big Gray. He was still alive, but injured and unable to move. I ran inside, got a bowl of water, hurried back and held it next to his head. This wild cat who had never let a human get closer than fifteen feet lifted his head and lapped at the water until he couldn't reach the bottom of the bowl. I refilled the bowl, let him drink his fill. Then I went and found a box and carefully lifted him and placed him inside. I was a little afraid he would try to bite me when I picked him up, but he didn't object at all. He just looked at me in confusion, as if this was all a strange dream that was not really happening to him. It was terrible to see Big Gray in such a state: he had always been the proudest and wildest of the neighborhood ferals.

I drove him to the clinic, where the veterinarian told me that Big Gray had a crushed spine and would never be able to walk again. It was time to let him go. She inserted an IV in his front leg and injected a solution of pentobarbital, and within seconds Big Gray had closed his eyes and all his pain was gone. His last breath was scarcely a sigh. Euthanasia is Greek for *good death*. It truly is a merciful death.

I try hard not to think about Big Gray, lying there day after day concealed in the shrubbery, unable to move while his thirst grew more and more intolerable. Big Gray represents so many things I cannot bear: nature's indifference to suffering, my own ineffectiveness, my hubris. Big Gray had crawled away to die in private, the way wild animals do. And in the wild, dying can take a long time.

* * *

The jay had finished drinking. She sprang down onto the grass and hopped across the meadow toward the bushes. She might be able to make another trip or two back to the birdbath, but soon she would grow too weak to hop. It was growing dark. The crippled bird would make easy prey for a cat or a raccoon, or she would suffer from thirst and die a slow and excruciating death. I wondered what to do. A broken wing could sometimes be mended, and the jay had no other wounds I could see. I decided I would take her to the native-bird rescue group first thing in the morning. They would fix her wing and then I could release her back into the garden. Surely this was the right thing to do.

The bird had hopped over to a corner near the wall, where I was able to catch her quite easily. I put her in a small cat carrier, covered the carrier with a cloth and put it in a warm, quiet room. I glanced at her one last time before I shut the door to the room. She looked much the way she had when I first spotted her at the top of the staircase: sitting very still, as if in thought. But when I went to check on her the next morning, the jay was lying on her side, her dark crest collapsed. In death, her dazzling plumage had grown dull, as if her blues—her indigo, her sapphire, her cobalt—had dimmed along with her life.

I sat down on the floor next to the cat carrier. Had it been a mistake to capture her? Maybe I should have left her alone in the meadow. Perhaps the jay had some other, invisible wound. I had no idea what I had done wrong, or even if I had done anything wrong. I felt futility settle around me like a great, sticky net. I would never know, just as I had never known how Big Gray sustained his mortal injury. So often we blunder in the dark, not sure if we are helping others or harming them, while the truth remains as elusive and curtained as the heart of a wild bird.

I buried the Steller's jay in the tangled shade of the clematis vine. Her body would decompose and become food for worms, and in turn the worms would die and become part of the soil and nurture new life. I find these thoughts consoling. There are no beginnings or endings for any of us, only a ceaseless cycle of growth and decay, rot and renewal. Every living thing in our world exists somewhere on this continuum of transformation. "Nothing is lost," Thich Nhat Hanh writes. "If we don't have this form, we have another form. If we don't have the cloud, we have the rain. If we don't have the rain, we have the tea."[20] I patted down the soil and atop her grave I stuck a feather, a blue feather that wasn't really blue at all, to mark the spot.

---

20   Thich Nhat Hanh, *Answers from the Heart* (Berkeley: Parallax Press, 2009).

SIXTEEN

Peaceable Kingdom

I was standing at the kitchen sink washing dishes when I looked out the window and saw a young deer, barely more than a fawn, browsing its way down the hillside. Spellbound, I watched Puck emerge from a clump of mule grass in full combat crouch. My cat was stalking the fawn. For one horrible moment I thought he was going to leap on its back and take it down, like a mountain lion, and I was on the verge of running out of the house, waving my arms and shouting. Then I came to my senses: housecats do not attack deer.

Still, I felt a little nervous. Did Puck know that cats don't hunt deer? The fawn turned and saw him, and both animals stopped in their tracks, inches apart. The fawn stretched out her long neck and Puck craned his short neck upward until their noses were touching. Deer and cat sniffed each other until, curiosity satisfied, they turned and parted ways. I breathed a sigh of relief. If only all of Puck's interspecies encounters could end so well.

Earlier in the summer, I'd seen Puck catch an alligator lizard. The numbers of these beautiful native lizards were in decline on the hillside, so I hurried to intervene, but I was too late. The lizard had dropped its tail. While the tail wriggled in the dust, attracting the cat's attention, the lizard made its getaway. That is how this defense system, called autotomy (*auto*: self; *tomos*: sever), is designed to work.

I felt a terrible pang when the lizard scrambled away, leaving its precious tail behind. It could take the lizard a year or more to grow a new tail. During that time, the lizard would not get bigger, seek out a mate, or lay eggs and make new baby lizards. I had a crazy impulse to seize the tail and run after the lizard, to somehow reunify the two. But that, of course, was impossible.

* * *

I once read an interview with Tenzin Gyatso, the Fourteenth Dalai Lama, in which he said that as a boy in Lhasa he used to feed songbirds. When the birds flocked to eat the seed they would attract hawks, so young Tenzin kept an air rifle to frighten the hawks away and protect the birds. It was, the Dalai Lama said with his characteristic chuckle, "a compassionate rifle."

The young Dalai Lama was inadvertently practicing the principle of harmonious association—protecting the birds and animals who coexisted without strife from the predators who wanted to eat them. This notion was pioneered by the late ornithologist Alexander Skutch, who used his own compassionate rifle to drive hawks and snakes away from his farm in the rainforests of Costa Rica. Skutch was aware that he was living a paradox—he tried in all ways to tread lightly on the planet, yet he was interfering with the natural relationship between predator and prey—but he feared raptors could have a disastrous effect on the wild bird population of his small nature preserve. Skutch pointed out that these carnivores didn't pollinate, didn't contribute to the food web; all they did was slaughter and devour other animals, sometimes quite gruesomely. "I would do all that I could to protect the creatures that dwelt harmoniously together, taking measures to remove those that disrupted this concord," he wrote.[21]

I felt deeply ambivalent about harmonious association. Ecosystems are intricate things, and meddling with them seemed wrong. Of course, we interfere with nature all the time: there is hardly a natural system left that humans have not tampered with in some way. And something in me resonated with the idea of a sanctuary, a refuge where violence was averted, where gentle, herbivorous animals lived harmoniously together—a true peaceable kingdom. What if Alexander Skutch, that venerable elder of the forest, was right, and peaceable kingdom was not an idealistic fantasy but an attainable and reasonable goal?

I once saw a red-tailed hawk fly through my backyard

---

[21] Alexander Skutch, *Harmony and Conflict in the Living World* (Norman: University of Oklahoma Press, 2000).

with a Steller's jay clutched in her talons and a flock of jays in pursuit, screaming in outrage. As the hawk rocketed right by me, I saw the black eye of the doomed jay rolling in terror. It was a dreadful sight. Yet there are few hawks here and many Steller's jays, so it was hard to begrudge the hawk her prize. She too had a family to feed.

* * *

Here on my hillside, harmonious association was complicated not by raptors, but by the presence of dogs and cats—my pets. There were no mountain lions, wolves, or bobcats here, so cats and dogs were the top predators on the food chain. Cats are born hunters; even when they are well fed, they have a strong instinct to stalk and kill. Dogs have an innate canine instinct to chase small animals—it's called prey drive, and nearly every dog has it. Dogs and cats definitely disrupted the concord and were a danger to wildlife and birds. By cultivating this wild habitat, encouraging birds to feed and nest here, providing water for animals, and making my garden so welcoming to my wild neighbors, I felt I owed them protection from my pets. Puck and Arrow were my beloved friends, the faithful companions of my days. I could not remove them. I would just have to manage them. I was sure I could keep things under control.

I got Puck a special bib that attached to his collar and made it nearly impossible for him to hunt.[22] He could still run

---

22   The neoprene bib Puck wears is available at catgoods.com. These bibs harmlessly prevent cats from catching birds, small mammals, and lizards.

and leap, but the bib got in his way when he tried to reach out and grab a bird with his murderous claws. That left the dog, Arrow, and she was always by my side. Almost always.

Late one summer night I opened the backdoor to let Arrow out into the yard. When I went to let her in a few minutes later, she wasn't waiting at the door. Stepping out onto the deck I heard a commotion at the end of the yard. I ran toward the sound, and found Arrow with her jaws buried in the fur of an opossum.

I seized Arrow's collar with both hands and jerked backward with all my strength, and incredibly, she released the opossum. I hustled the dog back into the house, grabbed a flashlight, and ran back outside. The opossum lay motionless on the ground. I shone the yellow beam of the flashlight over its head: its eyes were half-open and glazed, teeth bared, tongue protruding. I leaned over, hoping to hear even the faintest sigh of breath, but heard only the stillness of the night, crickets chirping in the background. In tears, I went back inside.

When Michael got home I broke the news that our dog had killed an innocent marsupial. I trailed after him as he went outside to look for himself. The opossum was slumped on the ground where I'd left it. It looked so pitiful that I started to cry again. Opossums may growl and hiss and bare their pointed teeth when cornered, but it's all an act: the bushy, pink-snouted creatures are the most mild-mannered of animals.

"Arrow's a dog; she's just doing what dogs do," Michael said. "It's her nature." He said he would bury the opossum in the morning, and we went back inside. But I didn't blame the dog. This was *my* fault. The killing of a gentle animal that was just going quietly about its business seemed like a terrible offense.

Just before bed, Michael went back out for one last look. When he came back in he had a big smile on his face.

"It's gone!" he said jubilantly. "The opossum is gone."

"Impossible," I said. "It was definitely dead."

"*Playing* dead," he said.

I ran outside. It was true—the opossum had recovered, gotten up, and walked away. I couldn't believe it. Of course, I knew that opossums played dead, but I never knew how convincing their pretense of death could be.[23]

"There's no blood on the ground or on the bushes," Michael said forensically. "I think that opossum is just fine."

I was very thankful for the opossum's miraculous resurrection. I felt as if I'd been given a second chance, to be more careful, more vigilant. Arrow would no longer be allowed to roam the yard at night unaccompanied. I would walk her on a leash every night. She would be completely under my control.

* * *

One rainy night the dog and I returned from our walk and started up the slippery back staircase. I'd forgotten to turn on the porch light and I couldn't see very well in the darkness.

---

23   The opossum's heartbeat slows, it drools and releases a foul-smelling odor, and it appears completely lifeless. The animal doesn't consciously control this behavior—it is an involuntary physiological response to a threat. opossumsocietyus.org